From Relational Hurt to Spiritual Healing

A.B. Bracewell, MS.

Love, Lust and the Lord Publishing

From Relational Hurt To Spiritual Healing

Copyright © 2018 by Adama B. Bracewell, MS

Published by:

Love, Lust and the Lord Publishing

5221 N. 8th St

Philadelphia PA 19120

ISBN: 978-0-692-99434-4

Editing by Donna Poole and Kimberlee

Kiefer, thepittsfordpooles@gmail.com

Book design by Tyora Moody, tywebbincreations.com

Contents

Introduction   VII

Part I   1

Betrayed, Beaten, and Bruised   3

1. Accept the Reject   5

2. Pigs and Pearls   9

3. Allow Me to Reintroduce Myself   11

4. Guard Your Gift   15

5. Are You for Me?   19

6. Hidden Royalty   23

7. Anything for Love   25

8. Left in the Wilderness   29

9. Scars   33

10. Side Order   35

11. Prodigal Son   37

12. Stand Apart   41

13. The Double Minded   43

14. Your Fruit   45

15. Self-Sabotage   49

16. Watch Their Works   53

17. You Are a Pearl!   57

18. Representative   61

Part II   65

Dead and Buried   67

19. Don't Look Back   69

20. Busy Being Busy   73

21. Out with the Old, in with the New   77

22. The Path to the Promise   81

23. Unrecognizable   85

24. The Wait   87

25. What's Your Type?   91

26. Play Your Position   95

27. Change   99

28. Get Behind Me   101

29. Hand to the Plow   105

30. He Will Bring You Through   107

31. It Takes Two   111

32. Letting Go   115

33. Jealousy   119

34. Joy Before Morning   123

35. Looking for Jesus   127

36. Man Up   131

37. Proper Priorities   137

38. Quantity vs. Quality   141

39. Romance and Finance   145

40. Who Do You Choose?   149

Part III   153

The Rise   155

41. Remove the Stone   157

42. The Sower   161

43. Battle Tested   165

44. Build Your Relationship on the Rock   169

45. Your First Purpose, First Instinct   173

46. Through the Storms   175

47. Launch Out   177

48. Hour of Temptation   181

49. It's Never Too Late   185

50. Private Testimony   189

51. Good Counsel   193

52. Serving Our Purpose   197

53. Battle of the Sexes   201

54. Due Diligence   203

55. Focus, Discipline, Hard Work 207

56. Impressions 211

57. What Makes Him Ready? 215

58. Love from Loved Ones 219

59. Stay True to You 223

60. Strength to Endure 227

61. A Call to Lead 229

62. When the Honeymoon Is Over 231

63. While They Can Still Smell Them 235

Introduction

From Relational Hurt to Spiritual Healing is inspired by my personal journey with dating, love, and relationships. It is an introspective look at how toxic thoughts, habits, and beliefs have contributed to the development of poisonous relationships, and how poisonous relationships have also influenced my thoughts, habits, and beliefs.

This devotional journey from Broken Soul to Soul Mate tells about the progressive change that occurs in building a healthier relationship between self and others, as a result of building a healthier relationship between self and God.

I have spent years searching for intimacy, acceptance, connection, and genuine love. My search has taken me on an expedition through pain and happiness, joy and heartache. The hurt and fear I carried from relationship to relationship was buried so deeply that it took years for me to realize that much of what I put others through was a reflection of my own anguish. As I began to develop a more intimate connection with my Creator I began to understand what true love is and how my method of searching for love and intimacy in the past was totally off track.

My choice to share my love lessons in the form of a devotional came as a result of the way God revealed these lessons to me. Through my own personal time speaking to God and reading his word I learned so much about my life in the area of relationships, love, and intimacy.

The scriptures that I use throughout this book speak about our most meaningful and important relationship, which is the one between us and God. The lessons I extracted from the scriptures are applied to my journey for love and a relationship between a man and a woman. This book should only be seen as a way that God spoke to me. This book should not be seen as a universal meaning or interpretation of the sacred writings. I would suggest that you seek a deeper spiritual and personal understanding of the Bible if you would like to experience its true power.

With this book I journaled my transition from being a broken soul that has been affected by relational hurt and toxic connections with others, to an individual that is progressively moving toward my soulmate by becoming spiritually healed, emotionally mended and mentally immovable through my beliefs and Godly principles. Although the book is divided into sections which are titled: *Betrayed, Beaten, and Bruised*; *Dead and Buried*, and *The Rise*, my journey has not been so straight and linear. The road has been bumpy and filled with detours and distractions. There have been times when I have lost my way, but God has always put me back on track.

It is my hope that my writing about the experiences I have had and sharing the lessons I have learned with others who are also in their journey will help us all reach the destination God has for us.

PART I

BETRAYED, BEATEN, AND BRUISED

Betrayed, Beaten, and Bruised

The effects of a dysfunctional relationship may leave us feeling unworthy, depressed, confused, beaten and bruised. We lose our sense of self and live in a state of fear and confusion. Getting back on track can be difficult, depending on the intensity and duration of the toxic relationship. It takes a toll on us mentally, emotionally, and physically.

Emotionally, we are torn down and worn out. The bruises may not be visible to others, but the brokenness in our hearts is real. Things like fear, anger, bitterness, and hate replace optimism, love, joy, and security.

Mentally, we feel confused, distracted, and sometimes delusional. After experiencing a relationship that is so unhealthy, it temporarily changes us for the worst. We start to lose confidence in our ability to make good decisions about relationships. We can develop a mental block against love as a defense against the mere possibility of ever feeling that level of pain again. Our brains constantly replay the negative messages we received.

After a while, we begin to believe those negative thoughts are true - that we are unworthy of love. A toxic relationship can leave us with low self-esteem, a poor self-image, and the inability to regulate thoughts and emotions.

In the case of a physically abusive relationship, we can be left with bruises that stay with us for a long time. We may feel lethargic. We might feel unsafe in our own bodies. We lose our sense of boundaries from having them violated time after time. Physical touch can be perceived as a threat. Our brain chemistry changes and we might even process positive relationships through unhealthy paradigms.

The good news is, we can recognize that this does not have to be our normal. It is time to make a change. We no longer have to feel beaten and bruised; we can to escape the pain and torture we have experienced. We simply have to be ready to take the first step away from unhealthy relationships and the first step toward a fulfilling relationship with God.

1

Accept the Reject

"AND IT CAME TO PASS, when the time was come that he should be received up, he steadfastly set his face to go to Jerusalem and sent messengers before his face: and they went, and entered into a village of the Samaritans, to make ready for him. And they did not receive him, because his face was as though he would go to Jerusalem. And when his disciples James and John saw this, they said, Lord, wilt thou that we command fire to come down from heaven, and consume them, even as Elias did? But he turned, and rebuked them, and said, Ye know not what manner of spirit ye are of. For the Son of man is not come to destroy men's lives, but to save them. And they went to another village."
Luke 9:51-56

Here, Jesus is preparing to face His destiny.

He is beginning His long journey to Jerusalem where He will eventually be betrayed, captured, crucified, and resurrected. Before He reaches His final destination, He will pass through other small persecutions on His journey.

In this scripture, we see He was rejected by the Samaritans and not allowed to rest in their village while on His long travel to Passover. The Jews and Samaritans had a strained relationship. The Jews considered the Samaritans unclean because they created their own way of worship, which went against tradition. So, Jesus was rejected simply for being a Jew and celebrating Passover in Jerusalem. The key here is to focus on how Jesus responded to rejection and used it to confirm His destiny.

As we prepare to meet the person God has destined for us, we will experience our fair share of rejection from others. At times, we will be rejected for what we stand for; other times, it will be for what we have done. On the other hand, we may be rejected simply for who we are. The chief lesson is to make sure we are growing from the experiences of rejection and not allowing the pain of rejection to consume us.

As we read, James and John were hurt and infuriated by the actions of the Samaritans. They were ready to pray for God to burn down the entire village, but we see how Jesus felt about that vengeful reaction - He rebuked them.

Sometimes, we let the hurt of being rejected control us, and that hurt turns into anger and bitterness which festers and grows inside of us, becoming rage. Holding on to the pain of rejection while on our journeys will stop us from reaching our final destination, so when God does bring someone special into our lives we may not realize it because we are blinded by anger and pain.

We must realize our destinies are not connected to those who have rejected us. As we read in the scripture, Jesus blessed the ones who rejected Him and then moved on to another village. He knew His destiny was not attached to those Samaritans.

Jesus did not beg the Samaritans to take Him in; He did not plead for them to talk to Him, nor did He cry because they did not want to see Him. He simply blessed them and continued on His journey.

I still experience my fair share of rejection.

Times when I open up, risk my heart, and put my pride on the line. I sacrifice my time, attention, and resources to be eventually abandoned, friend-zoned, or shut down. It is not a pleasant feeling. I had to come to the understanding that each rejection is feeding my perfection. It is God's way of making me better and pushing me closer to my destiny.

We are commanded to love, even when we feel rejected, persecuted, and mistreated. We must be able to overcome rejection, rebuke vengeance, kill internalized condemnation, and develop the spirit of love. When we learn that lesson and apply it to our lives, we will see how much faster God will bring us to someone who will love us that same way.

2

Pigs and Pearls

"DO NOT GIVE WHAT IS HOLY TO THE DOGS; nor cast your pearls before swine, lest they trample them under their feet, and turn and tear you in pieces." **Matthew 7:6**

Jesus' teaching is pretty straight forward. I think we understand what He means when He says, *"Do not give what is holy to the dogs nor cast pearls before swine."* Basically, we should be careful with whom we share that which is holy and sacred. We should treat it with respect and reverence. If we devalue it by giving it to the dogs and pigs, those who are unworthy, they will never recognize, understand, or care to treat it according to its worth.

When it comes to relationships, we should ask ourselves, how many times have we given our hearts, time, minds, and bodies to the unworthy? Do we repeatedly cast the pearls of our spirits to the pigs expecting them to treat us with love, only to have them trample and mistreat us instead? Those experiences leave us discouraged and fearful of moving forward in the next relationship.

Jesus is teaching in this scripture that we cannot get involved with the dogs and pigs of this world and expect them to treat us like queens and kings. They will continue to misuse us and trample on our hearts.

For this reason we must become more deliberate with our screening process. We have to know what qualities and characteristics are good for us, as well as the development of a healthy and loving relationship. We cannot get confused by what we need and what we want. We must put better boundaries in place. Our soul and spirit must rule over our heart and flesh. There have been many times when I have allowed my heart and flesh to lead the way, and it leads me in the wrong direction every time.

Our bodies should be considered holy. Our time should be held precious. Our minds should be valued. We must create gated fences around ourselves, so we can keep in the good and let out the bad.

Understand: we are more precious than pearls in God's eyes, so when it is time to give that which is holy to someone, we need to make sure they see us the same way God does.

3

Allow Me to Reintroduce Myself

"AND WHEN JESUS HAD FINISHED THESE PARABLES, he went away from there, and coming to his hometown he taught them in their synagogue, so that they were astonished, and said, 'Where did this man get this wisdom and these mighty works? Is not this the carpenter's son? Is not his mother called Mary? And are not his brothers James and Joseph and Simon and Judas? And are not all his sisters with us? Where then did this man get all these things?' And they took offense at him. But Jesus said to them, 'A prophet is not without honor except in his hometown and in his own household.' And he did not do many mighty works there, because of their unbelief." **Matthew 13:53-58**

As we take the journey of preparing ourselves for our spiritual soul mates, we will go through personal changes, we will expand our understanding, and we will experience growth as individuals and as Christians. We will also encounter many challenges and barriers along the way. We may think the biggest roadblocks will come from unfamiliar foes and the struggle of developing new relationships, but our biggest challenges to change may come from relationships and associations from our past.

As we read in the scriptures, Jesus' challenges came from people who knew His history, people who remembered His past, people who knew the type of family He came from. These individuals knew Him as the man He was and refused to see Him as the man He had become.

As we grow into the people we are destined to become, there will be people from our past trying to keep us a prisoner of our histories. There will be those who will not believe we no longer do the things we used to do.

Critics, cynics, and haters will ask similar questions to the one they asked about Jesus: *"Is not this the carpenter's son?"* Or in our case, "Is this not the girl who had a child out of wedlock?" "Is this not to the man who was a womanizer?"

We all have a history. We have done things we may not be proud of; we have made decisions that haunt us, and some of us might have reputations that are not very flattering. As we try to reinvent ourselves, develop better habits, make healthier decisions, and prepare ourselves for the one God has for us, there may be an occasional visit from people and situations God has delivered us from.

It might be an ex-boyfriend who tries to remind us of what we used to do. Or, it could be an ex-girlfriend who brings up how we used to act, or it may be a family member trying to remind us of where we came from. They are attempting to define us by our past, pigeonhole us in our history, and minimize our growth by magnifying the indiscretions of our former lives. Maybe we were promiscuous. Maybe we used to be an adulterer. Perhaps we dishonored our minds, souls, and bodies in some way.

These individuals will try to label us by who we used to be and the circumstances we used to be trapped in, but we cannot allow ourselves to be defined by our pasts. As it says in 2 Corinthians 5:17, *"Anyone who is in Christ is a new creation. The old has passed away; behold the new has come."*

I once heard a pastor say, "We change in a way that people cannot see." When we encounter people from our past, they may be blind to the changes we have made, but I can guarantee that our spiritual soul mates will openly embrace the new person we have become.

When you encounter critics, cynics, and haters, do not waste precious time trying to convince them you are a new person, because chances are they have already decided what you are to them, forever, with the expired outdated information they have.

Do not bend over backward to try to convince them. Do not be hurt, disappointed, and angry at their judgments. Invest your time and energy in people who believe in you, and keep growing, developing, and maturing in the way God directs you.

4

Guard Your Gift

"THEN SHE SAID TO HIM, 'How can you say, 'I love you,' when your heart is not with me? You have mocked me these three times, and have not told me where your great strength lies.' And it came to pass, When she pestered him daily with her words and pressed him, so that his soul was vexed to death, that he told her all his heart, and said to her, 'No razor had ever come upon my head, for I have been a Nazirite to God from my mother's womb. If I am shaven, then my strength will leave me, and I shall come back weak, and be like any other man.'" **Judges 16:15-17**

How do we navigate the bumpy and narrow road of being vulnerable and accessible to someone, but at the same time guarding our hearts? As we read in this passage, Samson's openness was used against him when he finally revealed his heart, strength, and gift to Delilah. He was taken advantage of and betrayed by someone he thought loved him.

This might be one of reasons why so many singles choose to stay single. The fear of letting down our defenses, leaving our hearts susceptible, and exposing our gifts can be terrifying. That fear can be a real barrier to developing a strong, healthy relationship with another individual. Though the fear is very real, we must find ways to conquer it if we ever want to receive and build relationships with the people God will bring into our lives.

It can be difficult to differentiate between who is really into us and who is only after our gift. But, as it was with Samson and Delilah, there are always signs we can look for that will help us better determine what a person is after.

Ask yourself: What are they focused on?

As we read in Judges, we see every discussion Delilah had with Samson was based on her discovering the source of his strength. She showed no interest in his family, his goals, his likes, or dislikes; she showed no real interest in who he was as a person, or who they were as a couple. She was preoccupied with his gift.

Have you ever met someone whose conversations are always focused on your gift? You feel they are not concerned with things that really make you the person you are, but are more interested with material and superficial things they see. Do discussions always come back to your sex, your money, your position, power, and prestige? This can be a sign they have ulterior motives and may be looking to only take advantage of your gift.

Do you feel like you're being emotionally blackmailed? In verse fifteen, Delilah says, *"How can you say, 'I love you,' when your heart is not for me?"* She is using blame and guilt to get a hold of Samson's gift. She is playing the victim to manipulate Samson's heart.

Is someone playing on your emotions as a way to reach your gift? This is something we should always pay attention to. Do they say things like "If you loved me..," or "I would do it for you". When we share our gift with someone, it should give us a feeling of joy, freedom, and fulfillment. We should not feel forced, manipulated, or pressured by guilt.

The final warning signing to look out for, is if they are only looking to receive but do very little or maybe no giving into you or the relationship. As we see in the interactions between Sampson and Delilah, it was all about her getting his secrets, getting his trust, getting the source of his strength. What did she give in return? She wanted him to be vulnerable but she never showed any real vulnerable moments. She wanted him to share his secrets, but she never was genuinely open with him. She tricked him into revealing his heart, while the entire time she was plotting with his enemies to take his life.

I have been the male version of Delilah in the lives of others. I played the mysterious role, while prying for every bit of information that I could to get to get her gift. I have been indirect with my feelings to manipulate her to open up. Yes, my hurt and inability to trust has caused me to hurt others as well. This is not something that I am proud of, but if I want to share my experience, I must share the full truth. It is my hope that you learn the importance of guarding your heart. It is not my goal to scare you or instill fear. However, I do want you to be wise and be aware of the deception that some use to get to your gift.

Learning to be vulnerable and at the same time guarding our hearts is a tricky balancing act. Our decisions about relationships should always include healthy input from our hearts and our heads. It is important to use our wisdom, our emotional intelligence, and our God to discern someone's real intentions.

5

Are You for Me?

"WHEN JOSHUA WAS BY JERICHO, he lifted up his eyes and looked, and behold, a man was standing before him with his drawn sword in his hand. And Joshua went to him and said to him, 'Are you for us, or for our adversaries?' And he said, 'No; but I am the commander of the army of the Lord. Now I have come.' And Joshua fell on his face to the earth and worshiped and said to him, 'What does my Lord say to his servant?' And the commander of the Lord's army said to Joshua, 'Take off your sandals from your feet, for the place where you are standing is holy.' And Joshua did so." **Joshua 5:13-15**

When God commissioned Joshua to take leadership of the journey to the Promised Land, his mission was to lead Israel out of the wilderness to rightfully claim what God had promised. It was not going to be an easy or peaceful takeover. Joshua had to fight many battles and face great challenges to take possession of the land God had promised to them. He became a fighter. His circumstances and his mission conditioned him to be hypersensitive toward any perceived threat.

A great example of this is found in the featured text when Joshua automatically jumps into defense mode when an angel of the Lord appeared to him brandishing a sword.

Joshua was on guard and asked, *"Are you for us or our adversaries?"* He did not realize the man was an angel sent to be an ally. He was there to be a partner to Joshua and was a blessing sent by the Lord. Joshua's propensity to engage in battle, and his failure to recognize an ally almost caused him to lose the blessing God had established for him and his people.

This instinct and conditioning found in Joshua is something often seen today. Some of us have grown so accustomed to fighting for what we want, fighting for what we need, and fighting to protect our hearts, bodies, and minds. We fight to get what we feel we deserve. Like Joshua, all that fighting makes it difficult to recognize when God sends an ally, a partner, and a blessing in the form of a strong, godly man or good woman, and, often, we find ourselves in a battle with them wondering, "Are you for me or against me?"

For some, it is hard to recognize a man or woman sent from God because a lot of us have not had the privilege to be surrounded by many.

Unfortunately, the lack of and/or complete absence of strong fathers, supportive mothers, protective big brothers, loyal sisters and committed husbands has made it hard for us to appreciate and distinguish between a godly individual and a dangerous man or woman.

A strong man often gets grouped with the type of man a woman has been fighting against and protecting herself from all her life. In those situations, the man sent by God becomes guilty by association. In essence, while her Prince Charming is doing everything he can to make that glass slipper fit her foot, she does not recognize it because she is busy watching and waiting for the other shoe to drop.

A good woman can easily be treated like all the previous negative women that a man has experienced. Those that were out to take advantage of him for their own gain. So when a good woman does enter his life he has no idea of how to work with her but instead he chooses to fight against her. He is conditioned to mistreat her.

In order to fully embrace the blessing God has in the form of a good mate, you must begin to change your thought process and challenge your instinct to battle. A strong man who is sent into your life will be there to support you but also to lead you. He will provide for you but also deny you some things. He will push you to explore but also protect you from dangers that you cannot see. He will profess his feelings but also tell you when you are wrong.

A good woman will be there to nurture you, but also stop you from making the wrong decision. She will help educate you on the things that you do not understand. She will bring organization to the chaos that you have been living in for all of your life. Do not always interpret that as control.

The important thing is to determine if their actions are done in love and the spirit of God, or if they're in the spirit of opposition or competition. Let's not be so quick to fight back against those things that go against our preferences, but learn to work together as partners. Embrace our differences and join together as one.

It is important to conquer our personal demons before we try to enter into a relationship. The most important ingredient in having a healthy relationship is to be a healthy individual. If you find yourself constantly on defense, guarded, distrusting, or allowing feelings about past relationships to affect your present situations, you need to heal from that.

A good man or woman may find it difficult to continuously be punished for another person's sin. Don't try to change on your own; start eliminating that spirit of rebellion by seeking help and guidance from God, loved ones, or professionals. Collaborative problem solving not only helps you grow into a better version of yourself, but it also prepares you for the partnership you will enjoy once God sends you a spiritual soul mate. You will then have the wisdom and discernment to know who is really for you and who is not.

6

Hidden Royalty

"SO HE ASKED JESSE, 'Are these all the sons you have?' 'There is still the youngest,' Jesse answered. 'He is tending the sheep.' Samuel said, 'Send for him; we will not sit down until he arrives.'" **1 Samuel 16:11**

Do you feel like you are being overlooked? Does it seem like all of your friends' numbers are being called, but you are not being noticed? Is everyone around you getting married, in a relationship, or finding companionship? Do you feel like no one sees the greatness you have, so when they search for their king or queen they don't even bother looking in your direction?

In the scripture, Samuel traveled to David's father's house searching for the next king. When David's father, Jesse, was instructed to call for all of his sons, David was the only one left out in the field to tend to the sheep. He was overlooked, left out, and totally forgotten by his father.

As singles, there are times when we find ourselves in a similar situation. We have all we need to be a great king or queen to someone else. We know we would be a blessing, but it seems like we are forgotten. We are steady in our work, faithful to our mission, and consistent in our ministry, but no one seems to recognize our greatness, just like Jesse missed the greatness in his own son, David.

But, as the story goes, despite being overlooked by everyone else, God had already selected David, and he eventually became one of the greatest kings to ever live. What happened to David is exactly what is happening in many of our lives right now: while people are looking past us, God is maturing us. While people are overlooking us, God is looking inside of us. He is helping us become that king and queen for the individual who will recognize the greatness we bring.

Don't get discouraged. Do not become impatient. Keep tending the sheep. Do not settle for someone who is not going to treat you like royalty, because you are lonely. When your season arrives, you'll be crowned as the queen and king that you are.

7

Anything for Love

"WHEN THE LORD SAW THAT LEAH WAS HATED, he opened her womb, but Rachel was barren. And Leah conceived and bore a son, and she called his name Reuben, for she said, 'Because the Lord has looked upon my affliction; for now my husband will love me.' She conceived again and bore a son, and said, 'Because the Lord has heard that I am hated, he has given me this son also.' And she called his name Simeon. Again she conceived and bore a son, and said, 'Now this time my husband will be attached to me, because I have borne him three sons.' Therefore his name was called Levi. And she conceived again and bore a son, and said, 'This time I will praise the Lord.' Therefore she called his name Judah. Then she ceased bearing." **Genesis 29:31-35**

Here we have Leah, a woman who was willing to do everything she could to make her husband love her. She yearned for Jacob to develop an attachment to her. Leah thought that having children with him would make him love her, but no matter what she did, she was never able to capture his heart.

Her situation is not much different from many people we might know, or maybe her story mirrors our own situations.

We too have searched for love in people who did not love us back. We have overcompensated to prove our devotion and feelings. We might have used children, money, gifts, or sex in the hopes we could change people's hearts and make them love us. We must realize no matter what we do, the love we seek will not be found if we do not change our focus, as Leah eventually learned to do when she made the Lord the object of her affection.

If the love of someone else is what we seek, we will never discover it until we begin to love God, as well as ourselves. What Leah thought Jacob wanted was based on her own insecurities and fear. She was so terrified and insecure over being less attractive than her younger sister, Rachel, and reaching a certain age and being unmarried. She knew that her father had to trick Jacob into marrying her.

Insecurities and fears lead us to lower our standards, our self-worth, and the blessings that God has for us. These distorted thoughts of "never being good enough," "never being attractive enough," or "not being young enough," cause us to look for love in places where it will never be found. We do more, but settle for less. We begin relationships where there is no love, and, in some cases, there is even abuse.

Are we willing to base our entire relationship on a hope? Do we hope the person we're with will learn to love us through our deeds and sacrifices, just like Leah believed she could do for Jacob?

For many, holding on to unhealthy relationships gives us a sense of security, but this is a false sense of security, and we think that this is the best that we can do.

Here is the antidote: We must become secure with our relationship with God first, and then with whom God made us to be. That is what will help us gain insight, erase all insecurity, conquer every fear, and grow the confidence and self-assurance others find so attractive and fall in love with. We must find it in God so that we never have to look for it in man.

If our main focus is on receiving love from anywhere other than God, we will always end up settling for less than the best. There is space in our hearts and souls which no human soul mate can fill. We can end up accepting negative treatment just trying to fill the void that exists in our hearts that only God can fill. We must develop a relationship with our heavenly Soul Mate before we are given our earthly one. We must come to the realization that this void can never be filled by any external force. Another person cannot make you whole. Broken individuals make broken relationships. Only the One who created you knows exactly what it takes to complete you.

By the end of the passage, Leah had birthed four sons for Jacob; it was not until then that she changed her focus and began to praise God. God blesses us with many things; that is how He shows us His love. We must use those blessings to love Him back, to bless Him back, to praise Him back. If we remember the source of our blessings and use those blessings to strengthen the most important relationship we'll ever have, the one with our Lord, then He will know we are prepared for whatever other relationships He sends our way.

8

Left in the Wilderness

"AS FOR YOUR CHILDREN THAT YOU SAID would be taken as plunder, I will bring them in to enjoy the land you have rejected. But as for you, your bodies will fall in this wilderness." **Numbers 14:31**

Throughout their journey to the Promised Land, the children of Israel tested God. They asked to go back to Egypt; they even tried to bring Egypt with them on their journey when they created and worshipped false gods. It reached the point where God was tired and frustrated with the peoples' contempt and distrust. God said His relationship with the children of Israel would wither right there in the wilderness. Because of their attitudes and behaviors, He was no longer with them.

God knows people only change if they have the heart to change. Regardless of the great miracles He had performed, despite the great promises He made, and all that He had tried to teach them, it did not matter, because the Israelites were stuck in their own wilderness, both literally and figuratively.

At times, it can be a challenge to recognize when it's time to leave a relationship in the wilderness. There are times when we try to teach, lead, and show the people we're with a new and better way of living, but they are comfortably stuck in their own wildernesses. When we are constantly trying to lead our significant others toward a life that they clearly do not want or are not ready for, we have to let those relationships wither in the wilderness.

So often we connect ourselves to individuals who are just like the Israelites. Maybe they enjoy toxic lifestyles we are not into. Maybe they have never been exposed to anything other than what they know, and they are not willing to open up to anything different. We try to teach them how to love, or we try to show them what it means to be in a mature relationship. Whatever the case may be, they remain stuck in their wilderness, and it is up to us to decide if we will spend our time, energy, and emotions trying to save them or leave them where they are comfortable.

In my life, I have been the one stuck and I have also been the one trying to rescue the stuck. I have learned that we can be encouraging, supportive, and nearly enabling, but we do not have the power to change others. An individual must be an active participant in their own development. When they are not, a decision has to be made. Do we leave them stuck where they are or do we continue to try to pull them out of the mud? I was once told, "Never waste the best years of your life, trying to bring the best out of someone else that does not want the best for themselves".

Some relationships will have to be left in the wilderness.

In the scripture, God told the Israelites the land they had rejected would be given to someone else who would cherish it and who deserved it. The same goes for us: we might find ourselves missing out on blessings and opportunities because the person we want to share them with rejects them. We cannot allow ourselves to be held back by someone that refuses to move forward. We have to gather the courage to leave them in their own wilderness, and we must develop the belief that there is someone for us who deserves and will cherish the blessing we are.

9

Scars

"AS HE SPOKE, he showed them the wounds in his hands and his side. They were filled with joy when they saw the Lord!" **John 20:20**

This verse is taken from the story of the resurrection when Jesus appeared to His disciples as the risen Messiah. He shows them the wounds in His hands and side where He had been nailed to the cross and pierced with a spear. On Resurrection Sunday, my pastor preached from this scripture teaching how our scars are a testimony and how Jesus displayed His scars, and as a result it brought hope, joy, and healing to others.

His message made me think about how we often have our fair share of scars. Some are visible, but many are emotional scars or mental wounds we bury deep and try to hide from others. These scars come from being cheated on, abandoned, abused, divorced, used, and mistreated.

The scars we attempt to hide affect the way we trust. They impact the way we communicate. They can influence the way we commit, and they tarnish the way we love. These hidden scars also hide a part of who we really are.

For years I have tried to hide my scars. I tried to cover up my imperfections, but all that has done is get in the way of forming true intimate relationships with others. My scars are a part of who I am. True love and intimacy does not love the perfect person, but it is seeing someone's imperfections and loving them anyway.

The scars we get during the journey to finding our spiritual soul mates are often seen as baggage, but they actually can be blessings if we look at them from the right perspective. Those wounds are filled with wisdom. Those lacerations on our hearts are lessons. Those fears make us more faithful. Jesus did not hide His scars, He revealed them to His disciples, and it was those scars that made them see that He was Lord. The scars that test us can be used as our testimony and can make us stronger; they helped to mold us into who we are today. Our scars do not make us victims, they make us survivors.

10

Side Order

"EARLY THE NEXT MORNING Abraham took some food and a skin of water and gave them to Hagar. He set them on her shoulders and then sent her off with the boy. She went on her way and wandered in the Desert of Beersheba." **Genesis 21:14**

When we read through the book of Genesis, we find the story of Abraham, Sarah, and Hagar. Sarah, Abraham's wife, was not able to have a child to carry on Abraham's legacy. So, she thought it would be a good idea to allow Abraham to impregnate her slave, Hagar. As we read in the featured text, Hagar ends up getting the short end of the stick. Sarah begins to hate Hagar and Hagar's child. Sarah demands both Hagar and the child be kicked out of the home. Hagar gets pushed to the side, left to wander, and is only remembered as a side note in Abraham's life.

Although this story takes place many years ago, it has an ending that it is very relatable now. Far too often, we let loneliness, desperation, and misguidance get the best of us, and we unknowingly, and sometimes knowingly, put ourselves in the same position as Hagar. Years ago, Hagar was called a concubine. These days, a woman like her is usually referred to as a side chick, other woman, or homewrecker. Regardless of the label, the outcome is usually the same.

When it comes to dating and relationships, it's never favorable to position ourselves as a side order. We should never allow ourselves to become the second and/or even the third option for anyone. We devalue ourselves; we lower our worth, and, eventually, we will be the ones left out in the cold. How long do we think we can live off the crumbs of someone else's love? We need a love that fills us up, not one that leaves us needing more.

The temporary satisfaction of occasionally having a warm body around cannot compare to the long-term pain and heartache of inevitable rejection. This might sound harsh, but it is true, and for your own wellbeing. Lowering ourselves to being a side order not only blocks the potential mate God has for us from coming into our lives, it also tarnishes us spiritually.

If you did not know this already, you deserve more than what you're allowing yourself to receive. If you find yourself in the same position as Hagar, I implore you to open your eyes and see the reality of your situation. You were created to be someone's main course, never a side order.

11

Prodigal Son

"AND HE SAID, A CERTAIN MAN HAD TWO SONS: And the younger of them said to his father, 'Father, give me the portion of goods that falleth to me.' And he divided unto them his living. And not many days after the younger son gathered all together, and took his journey into a far country, and there wasted his substance with riotous living. And when he had spent all, there arose a mighty famine in that land; and he began to be in want. And he went and joined himself to a citizen of that country; and he sent him into his fields to feed swine. And he would fain have filled his belly with the husks that the swine did eat: and no man gave unto him. And when he came to himself, he said, 'How many hired servants of my father's have bread enough and to spare, and I perish with hunger! I will arise and go to my father, and will say unto him, Father, I have sinned against heaven, and before thee, And am no more worthy to be called thy son: make me as one of thy hired servants.' And he arose, and came to his father. But when he was yet a great way off, his father saw him, and had compassion, and ran, and fell on his neck, and kissed him." **Luke 15:11-20**

How many times have we found ourselves behaving exactly like the prodigal son? We try to do things on our own. We feel that we do not need the guidance and protection of our Father, so we venture out and try to take control of our destiny without Him. This may not be truer in any aspect of our lives than it is in our relationships. We have a tendency to depend on our own desires, emotions, and understanding when it comes to seeking a mate. But without proper guidance we often end up making poor decisions and hurting ourselves.

Once we are equipped with money, degrees, good looks, and big careers we depend on those things to bring us a partner. We base our sense of self-worth in those superficial items. We no longer depend on our Father who gave us those things. We turn away from the one who truly makes us worthy. Much like the prodigal son, we find ourselves playing with the pigs, time and time again. We waste our gifts on people who do not deserve them and do not value them. We end up in situations that leave us ashamed, scared, hurt, and lost. We find ourselves stuck in unfavorable circumstances because we felt we could do it without our Father God.

We cannot do it on our own. If we are looking for our spiritual soul mate, we need Him, the creator of our souls, to guide us. We have tried to do it on our own long enough. We have tried to pick a mate by using our standards. We have used our rules, and we have used our wisdom. Where has that gotten us? Some of us have ended up in physically and emotionally abusive relationships. Some of us have ended up in relationships where we were used for our gifts or bodies, and have nothing to show for it.

For most of my life I thought that I could do it on my own. I tried to use my tangible gifts to attract what money could never buy. My finances, looks, cars, and education could never get me true love and intimacy that I sought after. Just like the prodigal son, I had to come to the realization that it is not too late to seek the Father's help.

It is not too late to come to our senses and decide we will no longer roll around with pigs. We can decide, right now, to get up and brush off all the filth left in our bodies, our hearts, and our minds from past relationships. We can turn back to our Father for guidance. We can turn back to Him for provision and turn back to Him for who He already prepared for us. And, we can be certain He will welcome us back with open arms and a kiss.

12

Stand Apart

"WHEN YOU COME INTO THE LAND that the Lord your God is giving you, you shall not learn to follow the abominable practices of those nations." **Deuteronomy 18:9**

This verse speaks about the need to fight against the influence of negative and sinful behaviors. As Christians, we often get involved with individuals who have certain practices, habits, or behaviors that are not pleasing to God. This scripture teaches us that we should not follow the abominable practices that surround us.

We sometimes enter into a relationship and become so engulfed by the flood of emotions that we allow them to fog our thinking and affect our decision-making. We become putty in the hands of the man or woman we're with. Those feelings of love, lust, excitement, and happiness can lead us to do things for and with that individual we know are not pleasing to God. But, Isiah 64:8 states, *"O Lord, you are our Father; we are the clay, and you are our potter."* We cannot allow ourselves to be molded by the behaviors of our mates that would pull us away from God's expectations.

Influence works much like a sculptor and his chisel. A sculptor is not able to shape a boulder with one swift swing of his chisel, but after several small taps, in calculated areas of the rock, the boulder will eventually be molded into that sculptor's vision. The influence of that sculptor's ideas and perspective shape even the hardest rock.

Negative influences tap away at us in a similar way. We may not notice any major changes right away, but small steady shifts in our behaviors will occur. It might begin with our mate influencing us to miss one day of service, or convincing us to have morning sex instead of having our morning devotions. We are told to stand apart. Our beliefs and values should be seen through our behaviors and habits. Claiming to be different with our words but acting like everyone else with our actions makes us appear unstable and hypocritical. We must pick a side and stand firmly.

13

The Double Minded

"A DOUBLE MINDED MAN is unstable in all his ways."
James 1:8

Be cautious of the double-minded, the wish-washy, the lukewarm individual, the one who wavers and suffers from indecision and commitment phobia.

As we travel toward our spiritual soulmate, the likelihood of encountering this type of individual is high. This kind of person constantly has us in an emotional purgatory as we wait for him or her to make a decisive move toward us. Beware of the type of individual who wants you to be exclusive to them but does not commit to you.

Beware of the double-minded—the individual who puts their right foot in but keeps the left foot out is playing an emotional game of Hokey Pokey. Be wary of the people who want to do relationship things but don't want a relationship label.

Beware of the double-minded, the inconsistent, incongruent, contradictory, and self-conflicting, for they are unstable in all their ways.

Through many years I was stricken with double-mindedness. I was the master of mixed messages. I would tell a woman that I did not want to be in a relationship, then act like I was her man. I would constantly remind her that we were just friends, then try to monopolize her time, attention, and her mind. I would sex her like I was in love with her, then shame her for developing deep emotions for me.

After years of having to deal with the self-inflicted pain, drama, and chaos that I created, I had to learn that being honest with my words is still a lie if my actions are telling a different story; and that I should not only speak the truth, but I must be fair with my actions.

14

Your Fruit

"EITHER MAKE THE TREE GOOD AND ITS FRUIT GOOD, or make the tree bad and its fruit bad, for the tree is known by its fruit. You brood of vipers! How can you speak good, when you are evil? For out of the abundance of the heart the mouth speaks. The good person out of his good treasure brings forth good, and the evil person out of his evil treasure brings forth evil." **Matthew 12:33-35**

If a person is known by the fruit he or she bears, how do we determine if the fruit comes from a good or bad tree? How can we tell when the fruit from the people we meet is too hard, too soft, underdeveloped, or not fully matured? How do we determine when a person is ripe or ready for us?

Many of us use the same techniques to test the fruit of a person's spirit that we use to check the ripeness of the fruit we grow in our gardens. We look for a certain color, a particular shape, a specific smell, or certain sweetness in taste. But, just like a cantaloupe which passes your visual test in the store only to be taken home where you discover it is bruised and rotten on the inside, the fruit of a person's spirit can surprise you if do not know what to look for.

Some people use the squeeze test when they are checking for ripeness. In the squeeze test, if you squeeze a fruit, and you find it is too hard you put it back because its firmness is a tell-tale sign the fruit has not reached its full potential. It is not ripened yet. That hard exterior tells us the fruit might be dry on the interior. It indicates the fruit isn't ready to release its true flavor and savory juices.

We encounter a similar hardness in some individuals who can't release their emotions. They put up a wall, a hard exterior, which prevents the true essence of their God-given beauty from flowing out to others. Many people use these walls as a defense mechanism, a way to protect themselves from being hurt. With this defense in place, however, they fail to realize that when they block themselves from letting out love, they are also blocking love from coming in.

Then, there is the fruit you squeeze that is way too soft. The slightest amount of pressure causes it to leak, split open, and drip everywhere. People who are like this fruit have allowed life to beat them down so badly they are now damaged. Any little pressure in their lives or relationships brings out their insecurities, fears, anger, or sadness. The fruit of their souls seems so bruised and beaten down that their every interaction is filled with anxiety, paranoia, and suspicion. The fruit they bear stops them from developing a healthy relationship with others because bitterness, regret, and hurt prevent them from having a healthy relationship with themselves.

As people, we are very limited in our ability to clearly determine if the fruit of someone's spirit is good or bad. There are many "boy meets girl" stories where, in the beginning, the man shows interest and attention to every detail of the woman's life. He is charming; he wants to spend every waking second with her, and he seems a little jealous if she spends time with others. To her, it feels like love. It feels like she's finally found a man who is truly into her. But, as time passes, his interest and attention turns into control; his charm turns into blackmail, and that hint of jealousy that once seemed kind of cute turns into abuse.

People are masters at disguising the true nature of their fruit. There have definitely been times when I was not able to clearly detect the fruit of a person's spirit. Times when I was totally blindsided by the behaviors of someone that I thought I knew.

If we want to discern what kind of fruit they truly bear, we must call on the help of God. He supplies us with the wisdom, discernment, red flags, and green lights we need to better see who a person really is. It is up to us to decide if we will bite into the fruit or put it back on the shelf.

15

Self-Sabotage

"THEN THEY TOLD HIM, and said: 'We went to the land where you sent us. It truly flows with milk and honey, and this is its fruit. Nevertheless the people who dwell in the land are strong; the cities are fortified and very large...'"
Numbers 13:27

In this particular part of the journey to the Promised Land, the Israelites were preparing to grab hold of what God had promised them. Moses sent out twelve spies to survey the land and bring back a report of what they saw. When they returned from exploring the land, they brought with them a message of fear and doubt. All but two reported that, *"It truly flows with milk and honey".* The other ten went on to say, *"nevertheless, the people who dwell in the land are strong; the cities are fortified and very large."* These spies allowed these negative affirmations of fear and doubt to sabotage their futures and destroy their opportunity to be blessed by God.

As singles we often do the same thing in our lives when it comes to being blessed with a loving relationship.

When we read this scripture, we tend to forget the times we have been one of those spies. We forget the times when we talked ourselves out of a blessing, when we self-sabotaged a promise by second-guessing ourselves, our abilities and our worth.

How many times have we met a great man or woman, and there seems to be some chemistry. They appear to have all of the qualities we are looking for in a mate, but then we turn into one of the ten spies? We begin to search for reasons why it could never work. We turn our focus to the list "dislikes" we conjured up. We talk ourselves out of the blessing that is right in front of us. We self-sabotage the situation by highlighting every possible negative about ourselves as a reason to explain why we should not and could not explore a relationship with that individual.

It is hard to say with certainty why we send ourselves these messages of fear and disbelief. Some might say it is a sign of low self-esteem. Others might believe it is the result of unresolved issues or a defense against closeness and intimacy. Maybe it is a way of testing a person's sincerity.

What is certain is that it is a way of getting in our own way, as well as getting in the way of what God has for us. It is also certain that, if we ever want to receive that blessing of the good mate our hearts yearn for, we must get to the core of why we have this self-sabotaging behavior.

As I conclude, I cannot forget to tell you about the two other spies that were sent to survey the Promised Land. While the other ten brought back a message of fear and doubt, their report was different. They stated, *"We should go up and take possession of the land, for we can certainly do it."*

They delivered a message of bravery, optimism, opportunity, and victory, and, guess what? They made it to the Promised Land. I suggest you do the same yourself: repeat, "I am a great catch. I deserve a great mate, and that's what God has promised me." It's the power of positive affirmation: if you send yourself that message long enough, it will not be long before you're living in that message.

16

Watch Their Works

"IF I DO NOT DO THE WORKS OF MY FATHER, do not believe me; but if I do, though you do not believe me, believe the works, that you may know and believe that the Father is in me and I in him." **John 10:37-38**

"Stop believing what they say and start believing what they do."

In this text, Jesus was speaking to the Jews who were about to stone Him. This conversation came immediately after He had just miraculously brought sight to the blind man by making clay from His saliva, rubbing it on the blind man's eyes, and sending the man to wash it off in pool of Siloam. The Pharisees accused Jesus of blasphemy and were ready to stone Him for what He had done. Jesus, knowing the people would not believe He was the Son of God from His words alone, urged them to look at His works to determine who He truly was. Jesus told them, "Believe my works."

As we continue our journey through singlehood, we can take a very important lesson away from this scripture that will help us evaluate people we meet in our exploration through relationships: We must learn to pay more attention to people's works than their words.

We are all familiar with the saying, "Actions speak louder than words." This phrase mirrors what Jesus was saying in this passage when He said, *"Believe my works."* The things a person does in a relationship are far more telling than the words he or she says.

It is extremely easy for people to just say what they think we want to hear to get what they want. There are sweet talkers, fast talkers, and bedroom talkers who know exactly what to say and how to say it to convince us they're telling the truth. But if their sweet words are not reflected in their actions, we have to question their words. Even Jesus said this about Himself. In the verses above He was saying, "Do not just believe that I am the Son of the Father because I say it, but believe because of the work that you see me do."

It is not always someone else's words that deceive us, however.

At times, we filter the words of others to fit the fantasies we want, thereby deceiving ourselves. For instance, if a man says he sees himself being married someday that should not be taken as him saying he wants to marry you. Just because he tells you that it does not mean you should begin mentally planning your wedding. If his actions do not show he wants to be married to you, his words mean very little. Do not take it upon yourself to add more to what people are saying than their words are worth.

John 2:17 says, *"So also faith by itself, if it does not have works, is dead."* Works is an action noun. When evaluating a relationship with someone, we need to make sure the words we hear are in motion.

17

You Are a Pearl!

"AGAIN, THE KINGDOM OF HEAVEN IS LIKE a merchant in search of fine pearls, who, on finding one pearl of great value, went and sold all that he had and bought it."
Matthew 13:45-46

You're a pearl!

Many of us struggle with the spirit of low self-esteem in one or several areas of our lives. We either feel like we are too much of one thing or not enough of another. These insecurities lower our confidence, sense of self-worth, and they can even tarnish our self-image. These feelings can also lead to the creation and the replay of negative messages that can become self-fulfilling prophecies. These insecurities blind some of us from seeing our true value, beauty, and rarity.

In the scripture, the merchant sought after fine pearls the same way a godly man searches for a good wife. When the merchant found that rare pearl, he went and sold all he had so he could possess that one pearl. When the man that God has for you finally discovers you, he will be willing to give up all the past relationships he had and all he once did, so nothing can get in the way of his destiny with you.

The key is that you have to see yourself as a pearl. If you do not know what a valuable treasure you are, my dear sister, he will never find it in you. I am a believer in the phrase, "If you knew better, you'd do better," and if you knew how a pearl is actually formed, I believe you would understand the loveliness that is within you.

My pastor, Herbert H. Lusk II of Greater Exodus Baptist Church, once taught that a pearl begins its life as a foreign object, such as a rock or piece of broken shell that accidentally gets lodged in an oyster's soft inner body where it cannot be removed. To ease this irritation, the oyster's body takes action. The oyster begins to secrete a smooth, hard crystal-like substance around the irritant in order to protect itself. This substance is called nacre. As long as the irritant remains within the oyster, the oyster will continue to secrete nacre around it, layer upon layer. Over time, the irritant will be completely encased by the silky, crystalline coatings, and the ultimate result is a lovely, lustrous pearl.

For a minute, look at the oyster as the body of God. When you came to God you were filled with irritation, anger, disappointment, and heartache. You had dealt with infidelity, abuse, divorce, and continuous let downs from previous relationships. Just as an oyster covers the broken debris lodged in its body, when you lodge yourself in the body of Christ, He covers your brokenness with layer upon layer of His blessings, grace, and mercy. His covering is evidence of how precious you are. His covering shows how loved you are. His covering is proof you are valuable.

Know your worth. No longer let things like low self-esteem, heartbreaks from the past or individuals who did not appreciate you dictate who you are. Know you are covered and protected with layers upon layers of God's power. You are a pearl.

18

Representative

"WHEN THE MASTER OF THE FEAST TASTED the water now become wine, and did not know where it came from (though the servants who had drawn the water knew), the master of the feast called the bridegroom and said to him, 'Everyone serves the good wine first, and when people have drunk freely, then the poor wine. But you have kept the good wine until now.'" **John 2:9-10**

In this scripture, we read about Jesus' very first miracle at the wedding of Cana in Galilee. This miracle marked the beginning of Jesus' public ministry. It was a very important moment, and it was also a great manifestation of God's glory.

Though the bridegroom played no part in the miracle, the master of the feast complimented him. He distinguished him from all others because of what he believed about the groom. The master of the feast said, *"Everyone serves the good wine first, and when people have drunk freely, then the poor wine. But you have kept the good wine until now."* Through Jesus' miracle, the groom was uplifted; he appeared to be a cut above the rest.

He was praised because a level of excellence and quality was maintained throughout the duration of the wedding.

As we go through our own experiences of engagement with people we are interested in, we should strive to display and expect consistent, quality treatment. There will be many individuals who will serve us the good wine in the beginning of the dating process, but as time goes on, and they seem to have us drunk on their love, their acts of kindness, romance, and attentiveness seem to slow down. Their infatuation with us dissolves. Their excitement for the relationship wears off, and what they serve us begins to lose its sweet taste. Their thoughtful gestures become a rarity; their generosity comes with stipulations. The chivalry isn't dead, but it's definitely on life-support, and they begin to serve us that poorer quality of wine.

In the beginning, everyone has the tendency to put their best foot forward. We show a high level of interest, concern, attraction, and attention. But, as time goes on, things change. Sometimes, that is part of a normal and innocent flow of a relationship; other times, however, it could be the result of intentional deceit. It is important to be able to decipher between the two and not fall into the game and trap that might be at play.

Take your time. The Bible says, "Therefore judge nothing before the time, until the Lord come, which both will bring to light the hidden things of darkness, and will make manifest the counsels of the hearts (1 Corinthians 4:5)." The purpose of dating is getting to know someone better - a date equals data. Utilize that time wisely. Take the screening process seriously. Find the focus to look past the surface of a person, and use dates to learn about what makes them who they are. Do your due diligence; get your questions answered and observe other relationships they have. Ask about their history in reference to family, relationships, friends, legal issues, and health.

There is absolutely no reason to rush through this process because if it is meant to be it will be, no matter the time. Most importantly, when the Lord sheds light on what the person is trying to hide, do not ignore the red flags. Deal with them like an adult instead of thinking that it will go away if you ignore it, because it will not.

Do not complicate your mind and emotions.

Romans 1:24 states, *"Therefore God gave them up in the lusts of their hearts to impurity, to the dishonoring of their bodies among themselves."* Sex can cloud thinking. It confuses the mind with emotions, and it makes it extremely difficult to make clear decisions on whether anything else other than having sex with them is appealing. There are countless stories we can think of which involve a friend, family member, or an acquaintance trapped in an unhealthy relationship because sex created the illusion of love. This is only one of several reasons why we need to practice abstinence when we are in the courting stage of a relationship.

The most important thing that the feast master did not know about the wine he marveled over, was that Jesus had ordered the entire thing. It was all made possible through

Him, and that is something we cannot ignore or be ignorant of.

If we include God in the process, all of the aforementioned things will be possible. Ask Him to order your steps. Seek Him in the person you're interested in; seek Him when you're out on a date. Seek Him when you make your decisions. Once He is present, He will make sure your heart, your mate, and your relationship stay full with the good wine He serves.

PART II

DEAD AND BURIED

"CREATE IN ME A CLEAN HEART, O GOD, AND
RENEW A STEADFAST SPIRIT WITHIN ME."
—PSALM 51:10.

Dead and Buried

A toxic relationship leaves toxic residuals. If we let them, the thoughts, beliefs, behaviors, and fears that were born in a destructive relationship can potentially change us. They may infect our hearts, minds, and spirits. Sometimes, we may feel like we can no longer trust, love, or be vulnerable. Those feelings do not go away easily, but they do not have to become a permanent part of who we are either. If we ever want to walk in the blessing of a healthy relationship, those toxic residuals must die. If we ever want to bask in the love that others have for us, those toxic residuals must be buried.

The heart cannot give what it cannot receive. Reframing the ways we view relationships and people can be a hard, long process, and those changes can only occur if we create a change in our hearts.

When Jesus died and was placed in a tomb, He took with him all the sins that prevented us from having a relationship with God our Father. They died and were buried with Him. Now, it is time for the things that stop us from developing healthy relationships with others to die and be buried as well. It is time to kill the past relationship pains, hurts, and barriers that are hindering us from receiving our blessings. We must bury the hate, frustrations, disappointments, and trauma we have been carrying. It is time to clean our minds, spirits, and hearts.

19

Don't Look Back

"BUT LOT'S WIFE LOOKED BACK, and she became a pillar of salt." **Genesis 19:26**

God had granted Lot and his family grace and favor. They were given an opportunity to be delivered from Sodom and Gomorrah, places of sin, violence, selfishness, sexual immortality, and other abominable behaviors. God saved them from a place and time that was unhealthy for their family. And then, Lot's wife looked back. Whenever God takes us out of a situation, a set of circumstances, or a relationship that is toxic and vile, one which is a threat to our well-being, we cannot look back.

The scripture does not explain why Lot's wife looked back. We are not told what exactly she was looking for or looking at. All we know is that when she decided to look back at a time, place and situation that were unhealthy for her, her fate was instantly sealed. We can try to deduce what might have been calling her attention by thinking about the times God delivered us from relationships that were bad for us, and we decide to look back or even go back to what He was trying to save us from.

Fear of the Unknown

Maybe Lot's wife was afraid of the unknown. Sometimes we are terrified to move forward because we don't know what lies ahead. We get used to our situations, and we would rather dwell in the misery of the present than to walk toward the hope of our future. We learn to make adjustments to the pain, we get comfortable with the mistreatment, and, before long, we begin to look back and say, "It was not so bad" or "it could be worse". But we must remember God has something so much better waiting for us and "not so bad" is not what He promised us. We cannot allow fear to stop us from walking away from a toxic past and claiming our future.

Overrating Time

Lot and his family spent a great amount of time in Sodom. That time spent might have been what pulled on the heart of Lot's wife and caused her to look back. So often, we place a high value on the time we spent with someone. Sometimes, the chronological time becomes more important than the quality of time. We hesitate to walk away from the suffering, and we keep looking back just because we spent so much time together. We put x amount of years into it, and we don't want to feel like our time was wasted. So, we look back. 2 Peter 3:8 says, *"One day is like a thousand years to God, and a thousand years is like one day."* So, when God is giving you an escape from a negative situation, that means the time was mismanaged, and He controls all time so there no need for concern.

Unworthy of Better

Perhaps Lot's wife felt she could never do better or get better than where she came from, so out of that feeling of inadequacy she looked back. Many times, we allow those same emotions to control us and to keep us stuck in a toxic relationship. We believe no one else will have the patience or desire to deal with us and the flaws we bring to a relationship.

People may try to make us believe no one else will ever love us or want us; they might tell us we are damaged goods. We may allow them to convince us to stay trapped, and sometimes, even once we're out of those kinds of relationships we keep looking back at them because we feel like we cannot do any better. But, we have to realize that it is all a lie and we must know God wants and has the best for us. Instead of looking back at them, we have to look forward toward the best that He has prepared for us.

We can go on and on, thinking of reasons why Lot's wife looked back. We do know for a fact that because she looked back at what God saved her from she missed out on what He wanted to bless her with. Negative relationships with people, places, and things can have a strong hold on us, but we must recognize it when the Lord is trying to liberate us from what is holding us back, and don't look back.

20

Busy Being Busy

"AND SHE HAD A SISTER CALLED MARY, who also sat at Jesus' feet and heard His word. But Martha was distracted with much serving, and she approached him and said, 'Lord, do you not care that my sister has left me to serve alone? Therefore tell her to help me' And Jesus answered and said to her, 'Martha, Martha you are worried and troubled by many things. But one thing is needed, and Mary has chosen that good part, which will not be taken away from her.'" **Luke 10:39-42**

Here we read about the sisters Mary and Martha. The scripture speaks about Jesus' visit to their home and the differences in their interactions with Him. Martha is described as being very busy. She seems to be frantically serving and so distracted by her duties that she barely has time to sit and connect with Jesus. The Bible says Mary sat at Jesus' feet and heard His words. When Martha complained to Jesus about all the work she had to do, all the tasks she had to perform, and how her sister was not helping, He responded by saying, *"Mary has chosen the good part which will not be taken away."*

When it comes to love and relationships, many of us singles act like Martha. We claim we want a good mate; we ask God to send us someone to share our lives with, but we are so busy being busy we allow our daily tasks to distract us from whom God wants to bless us with.

We are busy with work, busy with children, busy with church, busy with social organizations, and busy with school. We use those as excuses of why we cannot sit down and connect with other individuals on a close, intimate level. We put walls up all around us and claim there are no good prospects out there. Jesus told Martha, *"Mary has chosen that good part".*

If you are in your season of singleness right now, would you say your life resembles Mary or Martha?

Being busy can be used as a way to avoid others. It can be a defense mechanism used to fight against love, intimacy, and relationships. We fill up our to-do lists with many tasks so we have reasons not go on dates, or not call someone back, or not go to social gatherings. Some of us want nothing more than to connect with another person and develop a loving bond, then we use our duties as a distraction because we are afraid of becoming vulnerable. Some of us suffer from low self-esteem, and the idea of opening up to another individual is scary. But, I ask you again, which sister are you, Mary or Martha?

"Martha, Martha you are worried and troubled by many things." Jesus told Martha that what she called being busy was actually being cluttered, and that clutter was preventing

her from forming a close relationship with Him. Is the clutter in your life getting in your way of receiving the blessing God has for you in a spiritual soul mate?

21

Out with the Old, in with the New

"NO MAN ALSO SEWETH A PIECE OF NEW CLOTH on an old garment: else the new piece that filled it up taketh away from the old, and the rent is made worse. And no man putteth new wine into old bottles: else the new wine doth burst the bottles, and the wine is spilled, and the bottles will be marred: but new wine must be put into new bottle." **Mark 2:21-22**

Here, Jesus is speaking to people about the purpose and process of fasting. He teaches that anything fresh and new cannot occupy the same time and space with something old and unclean or it will lead to ruin. When we think about the discipline of taking a spiritual fast, we often think of refraining from eating certain types of, or all, foods.

When we fast, we commit to a change, a change in what we put in our bodies, what we put in our minds, and what we show in our behaviors. This process prepares our minds, bodies, and souls to enter into a new level of blessing. Fasting helps us to focus on renewing our relationship with the heavenly Father. When it comes to our relationships with an earthly man or woman, we seldom take the time to go through a cleansing of the old, yet we expect God to bless us with someone new.

As we prepare our minds, souls, and bodies for our earthly soul mates, a good relational fast is also recommended. This fast does not pertain to changing or stopping our eating habits, but it does require us to change any unhealthy relational habits we may have. If the blessing of a godly relationship is what we pray for but cannot seem to get it right, it might be because we continue to enter new relationships with the same unhealthy habits we had in the old ones.

The appeal and power of our old habits are incredibly strong.

We have the tendency to resort to what we know, regardless whether or not the outcome works in our favor. Changing old ways can be difficult. One of the things that make getting rid of the old so difficult is familiarity. Change is scary; it is a long process, and many of us are not willing to exercise our willpower in order to change. We can usually predict what is going to happen with the old and familiar.

Even when we predict that our old, familiar habits are going to get in the way of a blessing, we fall back into them anyway because they are all we have practiced to do. The old is effortless; it takes no discipline, concentration, or practice. An old habit is very difficult to stop, even when there is evidence that it will hurt, damage, and destroy people and relationships.

We can get so caught up in our routines and old habits that they begin to seem normal to us. We think they must be the right way of doing things, even if they are not. We know that if we jump into bed with someone, the chances are high it will ruin all plans to develop a blessed and long lasting relationship with a person, but old habits put us exactly where we don't want to be and can kill the chances of anything new from growing.

Some old beliefs, behaviors, and thoughts about relationships are inherited. If the people you looked up to taught you through word or action that the opposite sex can't be trusted, all men are cheaters, or all women are just sexual objects, then you will take that old way of thinking and interaction into all new relationships.

Ask yourself, "If God blesses me with the mate I've prayed for, will my old way of thinking, behaving, and believing be able to hold, nurture, and maintain a healthy relationship?"

After experiencing a series of hurtful breakups and toxic relationships I had to take a relationship fast. I realized that jumping from one relationship to the next had me stuck in a cycle of meaningless encounters, and I desired more. So I had to take a break from the dating scene and focused on improving myself and the one relationship that I had been neglecting: my relationship with God.

We all have old habits that get in the way of receiving the new blessing of a God-sent mate. We must eventually examine our old behaviors that are getting in the way, and add them to the list of our relational fast. How can we expect

God to bless us with a spiritual soul mate if we continue blocking His blessings with our own actions? How many times have you felt or thought something like this: "I pray to be married, but continue engaging in premarital sex. I want someone who can lead the family, but I don't know how to trust others. I pray someone will give me unconditional love, but I don't know how to open up and be vulnerable."

The examples are plenty because we all have struggles. Change is difficult, but knowing what God has in store for us makes it so much easier. Jesus taught us we cannot put something new over something old and expect it to last. Change is possible; we might have to change our prayer. We must identify our unhealthy relationship habits, begin the process of replacing the old unclean with the new and clean, then God will send us the one He's created for us.

22

The Path to the Promise

"THE ISRAELITES HAD MOVED ABOUT in the wilderness forty years until all the men who were of military age when they left Egypt had died, since they had not obeyed the Lord. For the Lord had sworn to them that they would not see the land he had solemnly promised their ancestors to give us, a land flowing with milk and honey." **Joshua 5:6**

A journey that was only supposed to take three days turned into forty years of wandering in the wilderness. Due to the Israelites' lack of obedience, lack of faith, and lack of trust in the Lord, they were kept stagnant in the deserts of Egypt, coming no closer to what God had prepared for them. God had made His promise, and all the Israelites needed to do was obey and believe to immediately receive it. But, instead, it took them an entire lifetime to receive what God wanted them to have because of their attitudes.

While in our singleness, we sometimes feel like we are stuck in the wilderness of relationships. Our love life feels as dry as the desert sand. It has probably been years since there have been any prospects, potentials, or even worthwhile dates. We get stuck in a cycle of wandering, just like the Israelites. We feel lost and confused, not knowing when we will make it through a wilderness filled with loneliness, desire, and boredom.

Stay mindful: there are times when it is just not our season for love, so we must learn to be content with our position. There are other times, however, when God has taken us through our season and is ready to fulfill His promise, but due to our own lack of obedience, faith, and trust in Him, His promise is delayed until we show Him we are truly ready to receive it.

How did the Israelites show their lack of obedience, faith, and trust?

There was a lot of grumbling and mumbling going on among them (Exodus 16:2; Numbers 14:2). This complaining was after God had shown numerous signs to them and delivered them out of slavery. This complaining is exactly what delayed their promise.

How many times do we find ourselves grumbling and mumbling about our situation? How often are we engaged in conversation expressing our frustrations with being single? Sometimes we grumble and mumble aloud; sometimes, it's a silent complaint in the secret places of our hearts, but God hears it all.

During the journey, the Israelites participated in many acts which displeased God. What are we doing as we journey toward our spiritual soul mate? Some of us try to create our own person to love instead on waiting on the person God created for us (Exodus 32:1). We are sometimes tempted to go back to who God just delivered us from, because we aren't patient and don't like to be alone (Numbers 14:4). They say that our attitude dictates our altitude, so if we are grumbling and mumbling we are only guaranteeing that we will be kept in a holding pattern.

The journey is just as important as the destination. The road we take, and the way we conduct ourselves along the way to our destination determines how long it will take us to get there. The path to God's promise of a husband or wife may not be easy or short, but it's the right road.

I tried to make my own path: I went in circles, constantly moving but not going anywhere. While on that road, my path was filled with fornication, parties, alcohol, and drugs. I couldn't even imagine the type of mate God had for me because I was stuck in my own wilderness.

I'll admit, the wait can get lonely, but let's not grumble. The journey can get boring, but let's not mumble. It can be hard, but let's not complain. Let's maintain our obedience, faith, and trust, and God will bless us with who He has prepared for us.

23

Unrecognizable

"EARLY IN THE MORNING, Jesus stood on the shore, but the disciples did not realize that it was Jesus." **John 21:4**

In this scripture, Jesus appears to His disciples after His resurrection. Jesus had just spent three years of ministry side by side with Peter and John, but they did not recognize Him when He came to them. That was because Jesus had gone through a transformation. He was filled with glory, and He had undergone such a magnificent change they were not sure if He was the one they used to know.

As singles, we can look at Christ's transformation as a model for how we want to become. We should desire to change our lives so drastically that we become unrecognizable to the people, places, and things of our past lives. We should strive to transform our lives in such a positive way that the people, places, and things from that one season of our lives struggle to identify us in our new season of life.

As we continue on our journey as singles, our hope and aim should be to leave behind past lives, behaviors, ways of thinking, and relationships that were not centered on God. In order to develop the type of relationships that will be pleasing to God and fulfilling to us, we must change certain things which hinder that level of blessing.

Through past our actions, affiliations, and acquaintances, some of us have built reputations that are not ideal. We must remember that just because God is forgiving does not mean every person in our lives will be also. There will be individuals who will try to define us for the rest of our lives by something we did in our past. It is our job to redefine ourselves so dramatically that those individuals who believe they know us and thrive off bringing up our past will not recognize us when they see us.

I know that I have changed. Some of the places that I use to frequent I have lost a taste for. Some of the people that I use to associate with no longer share the same interests as me. A lot of the activities that I use to participate in no longer interest me. Though I might have become unrecognizable to many people that use to know me, I know that God clearly sees who I am trying to become.

When Jesus rose from the dead, He raised us up along with Him. Now, we have the power to rise above the things and people that held us back and held us down. We are no longer anchored by low self-esteem, promiscuity, abandonment, abuse, or anything else that has been blocking us from developing the type of relationships God wants for us. We can become unrecognizable.

24

The Wait

"THEN BOAZ ANNOUNCED TO THE ELDERS AND ALL THE PEOPLE, 'Today you are witnesses that I have bought from Naomi all the property of Elimelek, Kilion and Mahlon. I have also acquired Ruth the Moabite, Mahlon's widow, as my wife, in order to maintain the name of the dead with his property, so that his name will not disappear from among his family or from his hometown. Today you are witnesses!'"
Ruth 4:9-10

In the text we have an excerpt from the book of Ruth, a very popular scripture among many single Christian women. It's so popular that the phrase "Waiting for my Boaz" has become a sort of pseudo-Bible verse for those waiting to be found by their spiritual soul mates.

Boaz was a great example of a godly man, and using him as a model for what you might want in a husband is a standard few can argue with. He was a provider, a protector, and godly gentlemen. There is no surprise why so many are "Waiting for their Boaz." But, let us look at Ruth's journey to her Boaz, which was just as important, if not more important, than her final destination.

For starters, Ruth did not wait for her Boaz. So, women need to be careful not to only focus on the Prince Charming arriving to save the day. Women must not forget the part of Ruth that details the long, hard preparation process she had to go through to finally receive her Boaz. That part of Ruth's journey often gets lost or minimized in the romanticized story. Ruth did not let her long journey discourage her; she did not let her experiences during her singleness harden her heart. Instead, she learned and grew during that time which prepared her to be the queen that she became at the end of her story.

Ruth had to experience the pain and grief of losing her husband. She went through the agony of a broken heart. Ruth knew what it was like to have someone she loved taken away from her. She dealt with the confusion, loneliness, sadness of a relationship gone unfulfilled, and being a widow.

My sisters, do not fool yourself into thinking that just because you love God that your Boaz will be hand delivered to you, wrapped in a bow. You will experience pain and disappointments. The pain you have already gone through from failed relationships is God's way of teaching you valuable lessons. Through those lessons you will become wiser about yourself and gain a deeper understanding of what He wants and has for you.

Ruth had to leave the comfort of her home and travel to a strange and foreign land. Meeting your Boaz might mean getting out of your comfort zone and learning to accept things, people, and situations you are not used to. You cannot allow your standards to become a hindrance to experiencing the world and the people in it. Ruth left her home and gleaned in the fields. Neither of those things was comfortable for her, but stepping out of her box was a step toward her Boaz. In order to live in comfort, we must first learn to get uncomfortable.

Ruth had to care for an aging and depressed mother-in-law who had just lost her husband and two sons. If you have ever dealt with a person who sees every glass as half empty and can see the dark cloud in every silver lining, then you know that was not an easy task.

In the first chapter, Ruth's mother-in-law, Naomi, says, *"don't call me Naomi,"* she told them. *"Call me Mara, because the Almighty has made my life very bitter. I went away full, but the Lord has brought me back empty. Why call me Naomi? The Lord has afflicted me; the Almighty has brought misfortune upon me."* I can only imagine how the experience of taking care of Naomi helped Ruth develop patience, compassion, nurturing, helpfulness, and sacrificial love. These qualities prepared her to be a great wife to Boaz.

Do not let the wait for your mate discourage you; do not let what you experience during your wait harden your heart. As you go through trials in life, love, and relationships, stay aware of the voice and lessons God is trying to teach you because your Boaz will be looking for exactly who God is molding you to be.

25

What's Your Type?

"SO IT WAS; WHEN THEY CAME, that he looked at Eliab and said, 'Surely the Lord's anointed is before him!' But the Lord said to Samuel, 'Do not look at his appearance or physical stature, because I have refused him. For the Lord does not see as man sees; for man looks at outward appearance, but the Lord looks at the heart.'" **1 Samuel 16:6-7**

In the text, Samuel was looking for the next king of Israel to take over Saul's reign. If we read a few chapters back, in 1 Samuel 9, Saul was described as being a very attractive man. It states, *"There was not a man among the people of Israel more handsome than him, from his shoulders upward he was taller than any of the people."* Samuel anointed Saul as King of Israel, but because of Saul's disobedience to God's word, God rejected him as king.

Fast forward to the featured text; Jesse, the father of David, was presenting his sons to Samuel because Samuel was searching for the next king, When Samuel saw Eliab, he knew he had to be the one. He had seen his type before. Eliab was good looking, just like Saul, and tall, just like Saul. Eliab appealed to the physical qualifications Samuel liked in a king, but God said to him in 1 Samuel 16, *"Do not look at his appearance or physical stature, because I have refused him."*

Just like Samuel, we often fall in love with a certain "type." There is a type God has repeatedly rejected out of our life, but every time we get delivered, we go after the same type again. Our type might be tall, dark, and handsome, or fair complexioned. They might have an hour glass figure, or be a nice dresser. Whatever it may be, do we find ourselves caught in a pattern of similar unhealthy and unfulfilled relationships because we fall for the same type? God is trying to teach us that none of the things we see from the outside are as important as what a person is made of inside. The moment we begin to imitate God's desires by looking at someone's heart, instead of basing our choices for a mate strictly on outward appearance, we might be able to see our spiritual soul mate.

As elementary as this concept might seem, some of us continuously choose a potential mate based on what we can see on the surface instead of the core we have to get to know. We are drawn to people for their physical attributes but don't take the time to see if they are as attractive spiritually, intellectually, or emotionally.

As I surveyed married couples, I discovered that many people did not marry who they'd described as their physical "type" previous to marriage. A huge reason for this is because most people get married based more on love, kindness, support, dependability, and compatibility, and less on complexion, height, eye color, and weight.

While being physically attracted to your mate holds some importance in a relationship, keeping it in its proper perspective is more important. If someone you consider attractive comes across as rude, insecure, selfish, disrespectful, or self-centered, after some time, do you even notice how physically attractive that person is? But, if you have a person who doesn't fully fit your "type" but who is kind, loving, patient, respectful, and has your best interest at heart, how beautiful will that person become to you?

I am sure that I have missed out on some great relationships because of my foolish inclination to go after a certain type. I struggled with putting my preferences of what I want in a mate before the priorities of what I need in a mate. I was once told, "If you keep turning everything that goes against your preference into a deal breaker, then you will never close a deal." Meaning that I would never find the true love and intimacy that I wanted if I continued to be fixated on a certain physical type.

In the scripture, God told Samuel about Eliab, *"I have refused him,"* even though Eliab had not said a word. This may seem unfair to Eliab, but could it be that God also saw another Saul-type king, just like Samuel had? The big difference was between Samuel's and God's perspectives. God looks at the heart. He sees the core of a person—the level of love, devotion, obedience, and integrity. Because we were made in God's image, we have the same capability to see the heart of a person. We must make that a priority as we wait and search for our spiritual soul mate. If we make the things God sees as important in a person, important to us, we can break the cycle of dead-end and time-wasting relationships.

26

Play Your Position

"IN THE SPRING OF THE YEAR, the time when kings go out to battle, David sent Joab, and his servants with him, and all Israel. And they ravaged the Ammonites and besieged Rabbah. But David remained at Jerusalem. It happened, late one afternoon, when David arose from his couch and was walking on the roof of the king's house, that he saw from the roof a woman bathing; and the woman was very beautiful. And David sent and inquired about the woman. And one said, 'Is not this Bathsheba, the daughter of Eliam, the wife of Uriah the Hittite?' So David sent messengers and took her, and she came to him, and he lay with her. (Now she had been purifying herself from her uncleanness). Then she returned to her house. And the woman conceived, and she sent and told David, 'I am pregnant.'" **2 Samuel 11:1-5**

In this story we see a king; we see a man who put himself in a compromising position because he did not take his proper position. As the scripture says, David was supposed to be on the battlefield leading his soldiers, but because he failed to stand guard and keep his heart and mind focused on his responsibility, he ended up in a situation which led to adultery, impregnation, and eventually murder. Just like David, we men often find ourselves in compromising positions because we fail to take our proper positions.

So many times we get caught in unfavorable predicaments. Sometimes it's intentional; sometimes it is unintentional, but we often find ourselves in predicaments because we were not where we were supposed to be according to God. We were not home with our wives. Our hearts and minds were not set on the people we love. Our eyes were not focused on our mate, and in a split second, temptation grabbed our attention.

Just like David's leisurely walk on the roof top led him to temptation, our conversations with a flirtatious female start off innocently enough but soon lead to temptation. A curious browse on a website begins with no ill intention but leads to addiction. An overly personal discussion with a female co-worker starts off friendly but leads to infidelity. If we are married, in a committed relationship, or looking to get married, we must stay mindful of the places we go, the people we talk to, and the things we look at because people, places, and things around us can lead us down an unfavorable path.

I have damaged a few relationships because I was out of position. I was with women that I should not have been with. I was in places that I know are not pleasing to God. I have been in the wrong place at the wrong time, and it was not always by accident. I had to learn a valuable lesson, that in order for me to receive and maintain the people that have been sent to bless my life, I must maintain my position under He that sends the blessings.

I once saw a saying that read, "The worth of something is not always measured by the price it cost, but also measured by what might be lost."

The next time you find yourself out of position, and you are in a place that can compromise your integrity and character, think about the people and things you could jeopardize if you do not put yourself back in the proper position. Ask yourself: is it worth it?

27

Change

"BUT IF THE UNBELIEVING PARTNER SEPARATES, let it be so. In such cases the brother or sister is not enslaved. God has called you to peace. For how do you know, wife, whether you will save your husband? Or how do you know, husband, whether you will save your wife?" **1 Corinthians 7:15-16**

The preceding verses speak about marrying an unsaved individual and how it is our duty as Christians to stay married once a vow has been made. But, the scripture goes on to say if the unbelieving partner decides to separate, they are free to go, and we are not held in bondage.

So many times, we get into unhealthy relationships, and we think we can play God in someone's life. We think we can change a person. We see a "bad boy" and believe we have the power to turn him good, or we see a woman with a promiscuous spirit and think we will be the man she will change for.

We see all the red flags, stop signs, and warnings telling us to make a detour, but we ignore them. We minimize the negative and exaggerate the positive qualities because we want to satisfy our own personal needs to be in relationships. We make excuses for individuals, and we turn against those God sends to offer good advice, all for the sake of relationships we know are not fulfilling or approved by God. Only He has the power to change people, and, even with that power, God still leaves it up to people to make the decision whether or not to change.

In what ways have you tried to change someone you were in a relationship with? Examine yourself, and identify if you have a strong desire to make others change, and then understand what motivates that desire.

28

Get Behind Me

"FROM THAT TIME FORTH BEGAN JESUS to shew unto his disciples, how that he must go unto Jerusalem, and suffer many things of the elders and chief priests and scribes, and be killed, and be raised again the third day. Then Peter took him, and began to rebuke him, saying, 'Be it far from thee, Lord: this shall not be unto thee.' But he turned, and said unto Peter, 'Get thee behind me, Satan: thou art an offence unto me: for thou savourest not the things that be of God, but those that be of men.' Then said Jesus unto his disciples, 'If any man will come after me, let him deny himself, and take up his cross, and follow me.'" **Matthew 16:21-24**

Jesus' destiny was preordained, and the time had come when He had to prepare Himself and those around Him for what He had to endure in order to fulfill His purpose and execute His Father's plan. Despite Peter's best intentions to protect and keep Jesus safe, Jesus had to deal with Peter harshly, saying *"Get behind me Satan,"* because, at that time, Peter's words were in opposition to God's destiny.

Peter was being used as Satan's mouthpiece. In the same way, God has our destinies preordained. With regard to love and relationships His plan for us has been established. When we arrive at the point where we recognize that destiny and begin preparing to fulfill that plan, there will be many places, people, and things we will also have to tell, "Get behind me."

There are guidelines we have to follow in order to receive the favor we hope and pray for. Most of us yearn to experience a great relationship, but there are things we have done or continue to do which get in the way of that blessing. We sit and wonder why we keep meeting the same type of people, why our relationships end the same way, or why haven't we met the one God has for us. As the saying goes, if we continue to do the same thing, go to the same places, and hang around the same people, we will get the same results.

There is a time when we have to stop certain behaviors. We need to change certain tendencies we have in relationships and the ways we engage with the opposite sex. When the things we do, and the decisions we make get in the way of us meeting our soul mates, we must learn to put those things behind us.

Until we get to the point where we develop a full confidence in God's plan and a true belief in His steps to building relationships, we will continue struggling with the same things that have hindered the release of our blessing. These types of places, people, and things get in the way of God's destiny for us, just as Peter attempted to get in the way of Jesus' mission. But, just like Jesus, we must see God has already prepared something better for us, and the things which stand in our way of receiving it must be put behind us.

I had to do it and I'm still doing it. A work in progress, there are so many behaviors and beliefs that I needed to put behind me. There are people that I have been involved with that I had to put behind me. Places from my past that I must leave in my past.

I urge you to evaluate yourself and to discover what you must change in your life. Begin the process of eliminating those behaviors, people, places, and things, and, with the help of God, you will be ready to receive what is yours.

29

Hand to the Plow

"JESUS REPLIED, 'NO ONE WHO PUTS A HAND to the plow and looks back is fit for service in the kingdom of God.'"
Luke 9:62

In the verses before this one, Jesus encounters a few individuals who express their desire to follow Him. However, when they were called by Him, they failed to take advantage of the opportunity.

One said he had to go say farewell to his family before he followed. The other said he would follow after he buried his father. Jesus' response to them was: "No one who puts a hand to the plow and looks back is fit for service in the kingdom of God." What Jesus is saying is we have to make the choice to be fully committed, fully vulnerable, and entirely invested in what is ahead of us. We cannot hold on to the past and be fit to embrace the future.

As singles, we sometimes act very similarly to the characters in this verse. We pray for God to send us a new love—someone who will treat us like we deserve, someone who is kind, spiritual, intelligent, and a bit edgy.

But, when God decides it is time to answer our prayers and sends us someone, we get cold feet; we begin to look back at our old relationships. We ask for a thousand signs of confirmation. We hesitate, never fully moving forward toward the blessing we've been sent.

Just like the unfit individuals who claimed they wanted to follow Jesus, we make ourselves unfit for the blessings we are sent by God when we begin to look for a reason to reject those blessings. Maybe we are looking back at toxic relationships. Maybe we are looking back to the fun we had as single individuals, or maybe we looking back at the pain caused by old relationships, and we become fearful. When we let the past distract us, we may miss what God has for us in the future.

30

He Will Bring You Through

"THEN THEY SAID TO MOSES, 'Because there no graves in Egypt have you taken us away to die in the wilderness? Why have you so dealt us, to bring us up out of Egypt? Is this not the word that we told you in Egypt, saying, 'Let us alone that we may serve the Egyptians? For it would have been better for us to serve the Egyptians that that we should die in the wilderness.'" **Exodus 14:11-12**

Can you imagine being one of the Israelites running away from tyranny of the pursuing Pharaoh and being led into the Red Sea? It sounds like the greater of two evils. Behind them they could see chariots and horses, mounted by spear-bearing soldiers who were coming to drag them back into a life of slavery. In front of them was a great sea of water with every kind of shark, whale, and sea creature slicing through the waves. The Israelites even spoke of going back to the horror that they left behind: *"Is not this what we said to you in Egypt: 'Leave us alone that we may serve the Egyptians?' For it would have been better for us to serve the Egyptians than to die in the wilderness."*

Isn't it shocking how powerful the stronghold of the familiar can be, and how strong we have to be in order to walk away from it toward the promise and provision we deserve?

When we read the book of Exodus, we might be tempted to criticize the Israelites because they wanted to return to the same conditions that oppressed them, but, before we judge them too harshly, we should look at times in our own lives when we were in relationships that were toxic, damaging, and dysfunctional. How many times, once we'd freed ourselves from that entrapment, would we would find a way to return?

The Israelites wanted to return to the abuse, exploitation, and struggle they had experienced with the Egyptians because it was familiar. When hopelessness, fear, and loneliness capture a person's heart and mind, the unknown of a better future seems scarier than the familiar brokenness.

We must understand we will never receive God's promise if we keep turning back to that broken place. God might not send a spiritual soul mate if we do not turn away from those toxic situations. If we are stuck in unhealthy relationships, and we don't know how to break the chains that keep us there, the Israelites left us a blueprint to freedom.

First, we must trust God has something better for us—a better life, a better man, a better woman, a better relationship. We must seek help; the Israelites needed the help and leadership of Moses. We cannot do it alone. We need to rely on friends, family, and those who want the best for us.

We must develop the courage to step into the unfamiliar and walk away from the relationships that cursed our lives just like the Israelites packed up their belonging and walked away from the crippling hand of the Pharaoh. Despite fear and doubt, we have to continue walking away.

Lastly, we need to trust that God will give the people who tried to keep us oppressed and depressed what they deserve. There is no need for us to be fearful or vengeful. Just as God held off and stopped Pharaoh in his pursuit, He will clear our paths and cover our tracks so we can receive our blessings.

If God can save an entire nation from their affliction, abuse, and slavery, He can do the same for us.

31

It Takes Two

"NEVERTHELESS, IN THE LORD woman is not independent of man nor man of woman; for as woman was made from man, so man is now born of woman. And all things are from God." **1 Corinthians 11:11-12**

In a society where independence is taught as the ultimate goal for people and when the rite of passage into adulthood is getting out on their own and supporting themselves, most of us value individuality and independence above all. We aspire to be financially independent. As children, we dreamed of the day we could move out of our parents' home. We listened to songs celebrating independence. Fathers teach their sons to do things themselves; women teach their daughters not to rely on a man for anything.

These teachings and beliefs are so strong within our society that the thought of being dependent on someone else is scary to many of us. We start to fear dependency or what some in the psychology world call "counter dependence." Though independence is glorified in society, when that attitude becomes a part of our spiritual and relational lives, it can be very poisonous.

The scripture says a man should *"Cleave unto his wife. And they become one flesh."* How has your need to stay independent gotten in the way of developing the kind of relationship that God wants for you? It is such a contradiction to program ourselves into believing we do not need a man or woman in our lives while simultaneously trying to build the foundation of a committed relationship.

If you enter in a relationship with the mindset that your mate is only a social, financial, or sexual convenience, and that you're good with or without them, you cannot expect to develop the bond that holds a relationship together. That spirit of independence goes against the spirit of partnership and collaboration.

I have seen couples who try to be with each other without being together. They live separate lives; they are emotionally distant and make decisions independently. Independence is the polar opposite of a relationship, so there should be no surprise that the two cannot occupy the same space. Mark 3:25 says, *"And if a house is divided against itself, that house will not be able to stand."*

You have not been blessed with the ability to achieve, prosper, and accumulate material goods as a means to declare your independence; those gifts are to be used to bless your relationship when you join with your spiritual soul mate. We need to evaluate our priorities and stop hiding behind our fear of relying on others. We might be used to doing things on our own, used to making our own decisions, and used to taking only our feelings into consideration, but, until we learn to trust and depend on someone else, we will have to get used to being alone.

32

Letting Go

"THEN PETER CAME TO JESUS AND ASKED, 'Lord, how many times shall I forgive my brother or sister who sins against me? Up to seven times?' Jesus answered, 'I tell you, not seven times, but seventy-seven times.'" **Matthew 18:21-22**

This scripture on forgiveness precedes the parable about the unforgiving servant. In the parable, Jesus tells the story of a servant who owed his master a great deal of money but was not able to repay it. His master forgave him, forgave his debt, and sent him on his way. The servant walked outside and saw someone who owed him some money.

When the servant confronted the other man, the man pleaded for patience and time to pay back the money, but the unforgiving servant choked the man and had him thrown into jail until he was able to repay his debt. When word of this got back to the master, he was angered by the servant's unforgiving heart and had him thrown into jail also.

Forgiveness is such a huge part of life for Christians, and we probably will not have to forgive anyone more than we will our mates. So let's prepare ourselves in advance.

Many of us have heard the saying, "I can forgive, but I can't forget." Basically, that means, I will give you a pass this time, but the moment you do something else I will bring it back up, or I will add it to your list of infractions. If we ever want to be in long-lasting, lifetime love affair with another human being we must learn to forgive, and, yes, forget. I know you are asking, "How do I forget what they did to me?"

This concept of forgiving and forgetting is hard for many of us to understand. Most comprehend forgiveness, but we still struggle with forgetting. This is mainly because we look at the forgetting part as a memory thing when it's actually a spiritual thing. When we are in a relationship and choose to forgive, we can perform all of the acts of forgiveness. We can kiss and make up. We begin calling our significant others again, and we even start spending time together again, but those acts mean very little if we are still holding a grudge in our spirits and keeping memories in our hearts.

We all have memories we would like to forget, but we cannot because the brain does not work that way. We cannot erase a memory on demand; instead, we must learn to erase the negative emotion the memory triggers in our hearts, so, in actuality, it is a spiritual forgetfulness. When we hold on to the chain of pain which links us to a past hurt caused by our mates or ex-mates, we can never reach the potential joy ahead of us as a couple.

In order to forgive and forget there a few things we must do. We must choose to focus on the good that our mates have done and are doing. Focusing on hurt only builds resentment. We have to communicate with our mates in honest and loving ways. We cannot pretend to be fine on the surface but hold anger toward them in our spirits. Our spiritual soul mates would like to do nothing more than to help us heal from the pain they caused.

Lastly, we have to remember we have been forgiven, and our penalties have been forgotten. With a sincere repentance, the Lord extended his grace and mercy to us over and over again, and we will have to also extend forgiveness to our mates over and over again.

33

Jealousy

"NOW A DISCUSSION AROSE between some of John's disciples and a Jew over purification. And they came to John and said to him, 'Rabbi, he who was with you across the Jordan, to whom you bore witness-look, he is baptizing, and ask all are going to him.' John answered, 'A person cannot receive even one thing unless it is given to him from heaven. You yourselves bear me witness that I said, 'I am not the Christ, but I have been sent before him.' The one who has the bride is the bridegroom. The friend of the bridegroom, who stand and hears him, rejoice greatly at the bridegroom's voice. Therefore the joy of mine is now complete. He must increase, but I must decrease.'" **John 3:25-30**

In the text, John the Baptist teaches a valuable lesson on how to conquer the spirit of jealousy in order to receive the gifts that are made for us. John's own disciples came to him, pointing out Jesus was there, baptizing people in the same body of water, and they made sure to tell John the Baptist that all the people were going to Jesus to be baptized, instead of coming to him.

As we prepare ourselves for a special person to enter our lives, how often do we find ourselves in a similar position as John the Baptist? We ready ourselves for a good man or woman through a variety of ways. We go to church and hold down good jobs. We are faithful, kind, and honest. We go to the gym three to five times a week. But, it seems like everyone else is getting blessed, falling in love, and getting married. It's easy to start to think, Why not me? What am I doing wrong? When will it be my turn?

Would John the Baptist have been right to feel a little jealous of Jesus' growing ministry? John did have more experience in baptizing. He actually was the one who baptized Jesus, and his name was even John the "Baptist." Baptizing people was what he did. John the Baptist could have looked at Jesus' growing following and asked, "What about me?" But, instead, he used this opportunity to teach us how celebrating others can lead to a blessing instead of bitterness.

John answered his disciples by first saying, *"A man can receive nothing unless it is given to him from heaven."* What that means is, no one has the secret to success, love, or a happy marriage; people receive their blessings from a place that has unlimited blessings. The fact that others find love does not lower our chances to find it also. The friends we see falling in love and meeting Mr. or Mrs. Right received their blessings from a place we all have access to. So we should eliminate the thought that they are special, and we are not. The only difference might be their faithfulness.

John the Baptist then said, *"You yourselves bear me witness that I said, 'I am not the Christ,' but I have been sent before him."* With that statement, John the Baptist showed contentment in who he was. We also have to be content in who we are, what we have, and whatever positions God has us in. We should never waste our time wanting to be someone else or wanting what someone else has. A person's relationship may look one way from the outside, but be totally different on the inside. So, be careful about what you envy, because you just might get it.

Lastly John stated, *"He must increase, but I must decrease."* That does not mean you should think yourself lower than a friend who recently met the one or those whose weddings and engagement parties you attend. It means we must learn to celebrate them and their blessings, allowing them to stand in the spotlight without letting our jealousy take hold. We need to show sincere joy for someone who has something we want.

Can you imagine how John the Baptist would have looked in the eyes of the people and in the eyes of God if he had tried to compete with Jesus and engage Him in a battle of baptizing? That is the same way we look when we allow jealousy and envy take control of our mind and emotions.

34

Joy Before Morning

"IN YOUR ANGER DO NOT SIN': Do not let the sun go down while you are still angry." **Ephesians 4:26**

They say time heals all wounds. This is true when the wound is immediately and appropriately treated. If a wound is not given the proper antibiotic, protected with a sterilized covering, and regularly monitored, cleaned and re-treated, it will become infected and infectious. As a result, something that may have started as a small splinter can require a surgical procedure when it is not given the proper attention.

In this scripture, the apostle Paul warned us against the danger of untreated wounds, unresolved issues, and incubated anger. He said, *"Do not let the sun go down while you are still angry."* When we allow time to lapse while we are emotionally wounded and angry with our partner, the results can be just as infectious and dangerous as when we let a burn or a laceration go untreated.

Anger and time are extremely dangerous when coupled. When we invite anger and time into our relationships, the outcome can be very destructive. As we prepare for our spiritual soul mates, we must practice confronting issues immediately and not allow them the time or anger to fester.

Time and anger are dangerous because they give birth to other enemies of our relationships. Time and anger bring along assumptions. When we cut off communication with our mates because we are angry, we leave room for negative assumptions. Our intentions might be to give ourselves space to gather our thoughts, but if those intentions are not clearly and lovingly communicated to our partners, and we just leave room for our mates to draw their own conclusions about why we're distant, during a time of frustration those conclusions will more than likely be a negative one. When we do not attempt to move toward a resolution in a timely manner, we give space for misinterpretation, which leads to further misunderstanding. That only complicates already sensitive situations.

Time and anger also breed resentment. When we let time and anger work together in our relationships, we have more time to think of other instances we made each other angry. Now all of our thoughts and focus are not only fixated on the original issue, but on past conflicts as well. We start thinking about the time our spouses forgot to pick us up from work, or the time our mates made us late for the super bowl party. Before we know it, our relationships seem like an unending series of bad and hurtful memories when that is actually far from reality.

Time and anger breed distance. The more time we spend away from our mates, by giving them the silent treatment, sleeping in separate rooms, or just being emotionally absent, the quicker that distance becomes easier to handle. As time goes on, that separation can eventually turn into habit and a new normal even if we desire closeness and intimacy.

The twenty-seventh verse of this chapter says, *"And do not give the devil a foothold."* The combination of time, anger, assumptions, misunderstanding, old resentments, and distance is a recipe for disaster in our relationships. They are tools of the enemy. These forces make us unhappy, lonely, and cause us to fall out of love. As believers, we cannot welcome or allow them into our lives and relationships. All conflicts may not be totally solved before the sun goes down, but through communication and love we can always take down anger.

35

Looking for Jesus

"FOR WE OURSELVES WERE ONCE FOOLISH, disobedient, led astray, slaves to various passions and pleasures, passing our days in malice and envy, hated by others and hating one another. But when the goodness and loving kindness of God our Savior appeared, he saved us, not because of works done by us in righteousness, but according to his own mercy, by the washing of regeneration and renewal of the Holy Spirit." **Titus 3:3-5**

Paul is reminding Titus of the type of attitude Christians should have toward others. He explains that we should respect authority, speak no evil, be gentle, and show humility. In verse three he begins with, *"For we ourselves were once foolish..."* This is a sobering reminder, a truth that Christians are not perfect. The only reason we even have the opportunity to work toward the unachievable dream of perfection is because of God's mercy toward us. This is such an important lesson to remember as we seek and find our spiritual soul mates.

In this era of "setting standards," "not settling," and "deal breakers," we can raise the bar so high for potential mates that no human could possibly live up to our standards. We can get so caught up in looking for someone who meets every one of our criteria that we lose humility and forget where we ourselves came from, or where we still are in some cases.

Many teachings tell us God will give us everything and anything we ask for, so when it comes to a mate we pray for someone who is the perfect height, has a perfect job, treats us perfectly, says the perfect words, and makes perfect choices every single time. Here is a news flash: none of us are perfect. We all have faults, and we stumble. Trying to find the "perfect" mate has kept many people searching for their entire lives. Jesus was the only perfect human to walk this earth, and there will never be another like Him. Sure, we might be able to hide our imperfections from others, but it's hard to fool ourselves, and we definitely cannot fool God.

Marriage is about two imperfect people joining as one to bring glory to God through their marriage. Somewhere along the line, we began to believe marriage was to find the perfect person to serve us. Our focus has become the "top ten things I want in a mate," and when we meet someone who has eight or nine out of the ten we dismiss them saying they don't meet our standards when God's standards are the ones we actually should be using to see if a potential mate measures up.

Stop trying to find someone who perfectly measures up to everything you want, and begin looking for someone who's striving to be more like Jesus. We should remember the miracle Jesus worked in us, so when we meet someone with a good heart and good intent we can remember God can work the same miracle in them that He did in us.

36

Man Up

"WHEN I WAS A CHILD, I spoke like a child; I thought like a child, I reasoned like a child. When I became a man, I gave up childish ways." **1 Corinthians 13:11**

I often read articles, see comments, or am engaged in discussions about what a "real man" is. Everyone has an opinion on what a "real man" is supposed say, how he is supposed to think, and how he is supposed to act. Regardless of what some might believe, according to the Bible, God has men assigned to the leadership position in their families. The trouble we run into is that all males are not men, and they are still trying to fill leadership positions without the proper qualifications.

The scripture says, *"When I became a man I gave up my childish ways."* In order for us to be the leader in the lives of our women or families, we must first lead our own lives. We must lead ourselves away from the immaturity and foolishness of our childhood and into the responsibility and integrity of manhood. This is not always an easy transition. Many of us are afraid to become men; some of us have never had an example of a real man in our lives, and some of us have only seen a woman play the role of the man, so we are accustomed to seeing a woman play the man in relationships.

Because I seek to lead my own wife and family one day, I had to look at my childish ways and begin to put them away. Through self-examination, I suggest that you do your own as well; I realized I had to do the following:

Put Away My Childish Way of Relating to God

Long gone are the days of childhood when I would grudgingly go to church because my parents made me. I used to sit there focused on going to the store after church, playing outside, or staring at the clock. I would pay attention to everything but the message.

To become a real man, however, I realized I had to strengthen my personal relationship with God. To accomplish that, I realized not only did I need to pay attention in church, but I also needed to read my Bible to become more familiar with His word, increase my prayer life, and seek through fasting and praying what God was calling me to do as a man. When the day comes for me to be the spiritual leader of my wife and family, I have to be well equipped to lead, and the only way I can do that is if I have a genuine, personal relationship with Jesus Christ.

Put Away My Childish Way of Managing Money

I had to learn to become a good steward of my gifts. Money isn't everything, but in this society it is an important resource. I had to learn the hard way about the importance of credit scores, saving for the future, and controlling my debt. As a child, I had no real financial responsibilities. If anything did come up, that was what Mommy and Daddy were there for.

As a man, however, I had to learn to resist the instant gratification of buying a new pair of shoes, or going out and blowing money on other pleasurable things. There will be a day when my income will be responsible for the livelihood of others, like my wife and children. Learning to be financially responsible was a lesson I had to learn.

Put Away the Childish Way I View Sex

At the pubescent age of thirteen years old, when nature began to take its course in my young adolescent body, I was hit with an onslaught of sexual hormones I had never experienced before. I was "girl crazy." I spent just about every waking moment thinking about sex, talking about sex, or trying to figure out ways to have sex.

As a single man, however, I had to understand how fornication, pornography, and being sexually focused damaged my relationship with God and had very real potential of damaging my relationship with my future wife. Furthermore, it distracted me from achieving personal goals and fulfilling my true destiny. Show me a man who is overly focused on sex, and I'll show you a man who isn't fulfilling his destiny. I had to learn to embrace the blessing that comes with abstinence until I am able to fully express my sexuality with the one woman who will be my wife.

Put Away the Childish Ways of Relating to Others

As a child, I was very egocentric. My major concern was me. I never put much thought into how what I did affected others. From my late teens to my late twenties my philosophy was "As long as I am honest in my words and actions, I cannot be faulted." It did not matter how wrong or how hurtful my actions were. I felt I was in the clear because I was honest. I would date multiple women at the same time, treat them kindly, be chivalrous, allow their interest and emotions to develop, but then I would fault them for becoming jealous or reject them for wanting an exclusive relationship. I felt I did nothing wrong because I told them I was seeing other women.

As a man, I learned an important lesson. I learned "Just because I'm being honest, it does not mean that I'm being fair." I learned I had to do right by people. I had to be sensitive to the feelings of others, and I had to make sure that all of my decisions were backed by righteousness and justice.

These were my childish ways, but if you want to totally fulfill your manhood, I strongly urge you to discover your own childish ways. Maybe you are still communicating like a child? Perhaps you still resolve conflicts like a child? Or do you possibly entertain yourself like a child by spending hours upon hours doing something like playing video games? If we, as men, desire to one day lead a woman and a family in the way God intended, it is up to us to identify where in life we still functioning as child and man up!

37

Proper Priorities

"INDEED, IN THIS CASE, what once had glory has come to have no glory at all, because of the glory that surpasses it. For if what was being brought to an end came with glory, much more will what is permanent have glory." **2 Corinthians 3:10-11**

In the scripture, Paul is teaching about how the glory of what was once beheld in the Law of Moses is not as glorious because of the greater glory, which is the gospel of Jesus Christ. The Law of Moses, the do's and don'ts and thou shalt's was the foundation of the Jewish church; there was nothing as revered, sacred, or important than to live according to the law. Then Jesus came to fulfill what was written in the Old Testament. He lived a life of greatness, suffered, and died for the sins of all mankind; then He was resurrected to take His rightful place next to the Lord. This gospel took the place of the law; the glory of the new gospel was so extraordinarily greater than the law that what the people once prioritized paled in comparison.

As we prepare for our spiritual soul mates, we too should be transitioning in the things we glorify. The qualities, behaviors, and beliefs we celebrated as unsaved singles should be replaced by what we exalt as saved singles now that we are seeking guidance from God about our relationships. Just as the temporary glory found in the Law of Moses was overshadowed by the permanent truth and splendor of the gospel, we must find the things that are important, permanent, and magnificent, about a God-sent mate, and put them in the place of the temporary, shallow, immature things we once held in high esteem.

When we were controlled by fleshy desires during our B.C. (before Christ) days, we glorified a lot of things that may have seemed fun and exciting at the time, but they definitely did not help us find someone worth keeping. We found glory in sexual encounters—the body and beauty of a woman, the money and status of a man. We were excited by things like partying all weekend, drinking and smoking all night, and taking someone home from the club. We all know what our particular vice was. As we grow individually and mature in God, however, we should make a shift in our priorities. If we want God to send us someone, we must understand we must be living within His will.

The spiritual walk of an individual will outshine a sexy walk. A person's prayer life is more glorious then their thug life. Their hunger for the Lord should be more filling than the finest dish of any fancy restaurant. The intelligence and wisdom they speak with should entice you more than any flattering smooth talk. The love and kindness in their hearts overshadows the swagger and coolness that used to attract you. Just like the gospel of Jesus Christ, these qualities are permanent. These are the things we can build a Godly relationship on. Hold them up, glorify them, and make them a priority.

38

Quantity vs. Quality

"AND WHEN THE DAY WAS NOW FAR SPENT, his disciples came unto him, and said, 'This is a desert place, and now the time is far passed: Send them away, that they may go into the country round about, and into the villages, and buy themselves bread: for they have nothing to eat.' He answered and said unto them, 'Give ye them to eat.' And they say unto him, 'Shall we go and buy two hundred pennyworth of bread, and give them to eat?' He saith unto them, 'How many loaves have ye? Go and see.' And when they knew, they say, 'five, and two fishes.' And he commanded them to make all sit down by companies upon the green grass. And they sat down in ranks, by hundreds, and by fifties. And when he had taken the five loaves and the two fishes, he looked up to heaven, and blessed, and brake the loaves, and gave them to his disciples to set before them; and the two fishes divided he among them all. And they did all eat, and were filled." **Mark 6:35-42**

We often believe that, in order to satisfy our craving for love and companionship and to meet that special one, we have to entertain many. We feel the supply must equal the demand. We convince ourselves the demand cannot be met by a single individual and having a parade of potentials to keep us occupied and entertained is the most effective way to connect with and find the one individual we will build with.

As we see in the scripture above, the disciples asked Jesus, *"Shall we go and buy two hundred pennyworth of bread, and give them to eat?"* They thought because there was a huge, hungry crowd, there needed to be a huge supply. They were thinking about the quantity of demand in front of them, and they forgot about the quality of the man who was beside them.

Human nature is weak. We are easily driven by lust and quickly fall to temptation. When we combine our weakness with our desire for love, we are headed for danger. We look for this emptiness to be filled by different people in different ways. We think increasing the quantity is the cure. We cannot have the mentality of the disciples. We must remember Who is by our side. We must understand that when something is blessed by God, He does not need much to make a miracle. He can satisfy our hunger with the one He has already prepared for us, and that one will satisfy our hunger far better than the many we could find on our own.

The choice to go for quantity over quality is usually a result of our level of understanding of what God has for us. When we are going for quantity, we more likely are living our lives by worldly expectations and not the Lord's standards. Not only are we clueless about what God has for us, but we have no idea what we want for ourselves, so we look to satisfy that hunger in a number of women and men, accepting whatever they have to offer because we don't know what we want. If you have a desire to find love, companionship, and connection, and if you starve for a fulfilling relationship with one special individual, you can't choose to go for quantity over quality. Going for quantity shows a lack of developmental, emotional, and spiritual maturity.

For those of us who have done our fair share of casual dating, hopefully we have learned exactly what we want in a mate. Hopefully, it has taught us to become more selective with who we give our time, attention, and energy to, so we can transition from dating casually to dating with a purpose.

Lastly, the choice to go for quantity over quality shows we are trying to feed our own hunger and not allowing God to satisfy our appetite. We are weak. The flesh is lustful, and our minds are very impressionable; if we try to satisfy our hunger for companionship without seeking guidance from God, our thirst will never be properly quenched.

39

Romance and Finance

"THEN JESUS BEHOLDING HIM LOVED HIM, and said unto him, 'One thing thou lackest: go thy way, sell whatsoever thou hast, and give to the poor, and thou shalt have treasure in heaven: and come, take up the cross, and follow me.' And he was sad at that saying, and went away grieved: for he had great possessions. And Jesus looked round about, and saith unto his disciples, 'How hardly shall they that have riches enter into the kingdom of God!' And the disciples were astonished at his words. But Jesus answereth again, and saith unto them, 'Children, how hard is it for them that trust in riches to enter into the kingdom of God! It is easier for a camel to go through the eye of a needle, than for a rich man to enter into the kingdom of God.'" **Mark 10:21-24**

Here we have the familiar story of the rich man who sadly walked away from something he deeply wanted. This man sought out Jesus to inquire how to inherit eternal life. He felt he had done everything right, kept all the commandments, and lived a righteous and faithful life. He was confident he could follow Christ until Jesus gave him one last requirement to attain the eternal life he desired. He was told to sell all he had and give his possessions to the poor to receive the treasure God had for him in heaven. Jesus' instruction to sacrifice all the rich young man had accomplished was too much for him, and he walked away from the life he had thought he truly wanted.

As Christians, there are times when be behave very similarly to this young man. We can allow our worldly possessions, achievements, accomplishments, and accolades to become the reason we walk away from the life we seek after. We are very hesitant to share our riches, let go of our possessions, or sacrifice what we have accomplished. We are saddened and scared by the mere thought of altering our way of living in order to raise our standard of living. There is no area this comes into play more than in our relationships.

Finances are among the top reasons why half of marriages end in divorce. Prenuptial agreements have become a serious requirement or consideration in many marriages. With advancements in technology, it has become more common to meet and maintain a relationship with a potential future spouse who lives hundreds of miles away. However, if that relationship moves beyond a courtship into something more serious, someone will have to leave the security of his or her job, home, business, and profession in order to make getting married a possibility. As we prepare ourselves for God's blessing of a husband or wife, we must keep in mind the sacrifices we might have to make. We have to determine if we are willing to make those kinds of sacrifices.

The rich man thought he was fully prepared to enter into the blessing of eternal life with God. He felt he had done everything correctly, but Jesus was not interested in whether the rich young ruler had kept every commandment. Jesus already knew His mission on earth was to pay, through His crucifixion, for every commandment the rich man had ever broken. Jesus was concerned about where the rich man's trust was. That determined whether or not the rich young ruler received the blessing he sought after.

Do we fully trust God to send us what we pray for? Are we hesitant to lose total control but seek the blessing of a marriage? Where do finances rank on your list of importance with regard to marriage? What are your ideas and thoughts on love and finances? How would you discuss this with your perspective mate? Is the subject of money big enough to turn you away from the blessing you want, or do you believe with God all things are possible? We must meditate on these questions as we ask God to send us a mate.

40

Who Do You Choose?

"DO YOU WANT ME TO RELEASE TO YOU the king of the Jews?' asked Pilate, knowing it was out of self-interest that the chief priests had handed Jesus over to him. But the chief priests stirred up the crowd to have Pilate release Barabbas instead." **Mark 15:9-11**

In the text, Jesus had been handed over to Pilate for him to make a decision on what Jesus' fate would be. Back then, it was customary during the Passover Feast for the people to vote for one prisoner to be released and sent back into the community. That day, Jesus, a righteous, innocent man stood next to Barabbas, a rebel and known murderer, waiting for a verdict from the crowd. Barabbas was set free.

As we read this familiar story of the crucifixion, it's easy to feel anger and disbelief at the rowdy crowd and the decision they made. But if we think about it, there have been times we were faced with similar choices. We had to decide who we were going to allow into our lives, and who we were going to send away.

Just like the crowd in Mark 15, we have a choice who we want to walk with, talk with, and share our space and time with. Who do we repeatedly choose? Do we pick the good and grounded individuals who try to live their lives as righteously as possible? Or do we choose the Barabbases of the world who entice our excitement and cater to our carnal desires even though we know they go against what we believe is godly and good?

As we look at the crowd in these verses, we can identify some of the reasons why they chose Barabbas over Jesus and by doing that we can better understand and be aware of the choices we make with the people we allow into our lives.

In the text it says, *"But the chief priest stirred up the crowd to have him release to them Barabbas."* An authoritative influence urged the crowd to make a choice. So I ask, what's influencing the choices we make in people? Do we trust in outside appearances? Is the media's portrayal of what is good and desirable influencing the type of man or woman we allow into our lives? Are we being guided by friends' opinions? Are we following the lead of what we see everyone like on social media? We must be careful who we allow to influence us and our choices. We cannot try to impress others with the people we choose. We also cannot choose people in order to feel validated by others. We must learn the things that impress God and allow those things to be what influence our decisions.

Ignorance was possibly another reason why the crowd chose Barabbas over Jesus. They were not familiar with a man like Jesus, but because they were living in a sinful time, Barabbas was a familiar figure to them. Just like the crowd, we to tend to make our choices of people based on what we are familiar with. We default back to the types of people we grew up around, are used to dating, or the type of relationships we grew up observing. Familiarity can be very dangerous when the things we are familiar with are not healthy. There are times when we have to break the mold and decide not to pick the same type of man or woman we were just delivered from in our last relationship. We can look back at the rowdy crowd and think Jesus was obviously the right choice, but we are faced with similar decisions every day in our lives, and we do not always go the way of Jesus.

Lastly, but most important, the crowd's decision was influenced by God. It was a part God's plan. In the same way, our choices are all a part of God's plan. No matter how good or how bad our choices have been, no matter what type of woman or man we have set free to roam in our space, Romans 8:28 tell us that it works out for the good for those that love the Lord and are called according to His purpose.

I can write an entire book about the unwise choices I have made with people and relationships, and how so many of my choices used to be solely lead by emotion and lust, not by God. This is a constant struggle that I have gotten much better with over time. Everything that we get or do not get in life is a direct result of the choices we make. It is time for us to start making better ones.

It doesn't matter if we have chosen the wrong people in the past. What is important now is that we learn the lesson God is trying to teach us through our free will to choose. We should realize what we've gone through has all been a part of God's plan for getting us ready for who He has already prepared for us.

PART III

THE RISE

"TAKE DELIGHT IN THE LORD AND HE WILL GIVE
YOU THE DESIRES OF YOUR HEART."
—PSALM 37:4.

The Rise

We all hope we will be ready when God brings the one He has prepared for us into our lives. After we have been betrayed, beaten, and bruised, and have buried the toxic residue of the past, it is time for us to rise. It is time to be healed and move forward. The experiences we have gone through have served as important life lessons. We now know who we are, what we need, and what God desires for our future. It is up to us to begin to walk in His promises.

Rise above the fears of heartache.

It is time to rise above the pain in our souls. If we want the healthy relationship we have prayed for, we must learn how to give and receive love. It is time to rise above bitterness, anger, and resentment so we can receive what our heart truly desires. It is time to rise above embarrassment, critics, and poor decisions we have allowed to define our lives. It is time to redefine ourselves with God's dictionary, and not allow those who have tried to break us to define who we are. It is time to rise up with confidence that we will be protected, and the assurance that everything works together for the good, no matter how bad things may seem.

When we are able to rise above the things we have experienced, we can freely love others because we have learned to find in God the love we once looked for in people. We no longer need validation from others. We are no longer held down by the weight of our past issues. It is time to rise up and start a new beginning.

"Brethren, I do not regard myself as having laid hold of it yet; but one thing I do: forgetting what lies behind and reaching forward to what lies ahead."—Philippians 3:1

41

Remove the Stone

"'TAKE AWAY THE STONE,' he said. 'But, Lord,' said Martha, the sister of the dead man, 'by this time there is a bad odor, for he has been there four days.' Then Jesus said, 'Did I not tell you that if you believe, you will see the glory of God?' So they took away the stone." **John 11:39-41**

In order for Jesus to create a miracle in the lives of Lazarus and his family, the stone had to be taken away. This stone was a barrier to their blessing. It stood in the way and had to be removed so they could experience the full glory of God. Similarly, we singles have stones in our lives which block us from receiving the blessings we desire. Whether it is the blessing of love, intimacy, or companionship and stability, our stones must be removed before we can fully love others, fully love ourselves, and fully love God.

We carry around stones of anger, fear, resentment, and pain. Often times, we become stones. Our hearts are hardened; we are emotionally detached and mentally withdrawn. These stones must be removed. We cannot receive or give love if we have a stone blocking our hearts, and we definitely cannot receive or give love if we allow life experiences to harden our hearts.

I carried around a heavy stone. My stone always stopped me from being totally vulnerable in my relationships. I have always been good with encouraging others to reveal their whole heart, while I only partially opened up my own. That mysterious side of me worked in my favor plenty of times because women would often try harder to win my heart, which in turn fed my own ego.

After a while I realized that my mysterious personality was actually a stone of poor expression and communication. My stone blocked me from fully releasing love, gratitude, and compassion toward others. My stone came from growing up in a home and community where your emotions were not frequently expressed. At home, words like "I love you" or warm embraces were a rarity; and in my community showing any emotion other than anger and rage could make you susceptible to being victimized. That was a heavy stone that I carried.

This stone stopped me from complimenting someone when they needed it most, or hugging them when they needed a warm embrace. I had to remove that stone, and to be honest it is still being moved. Having my son Jeovanni has definitely helped that stone to move a much further distance away from my heart. Learning to express my love for him and to him has given me a real understanding of how Jesus loves me, because I will sacrifice everything for my boy. Through the experience of God's love and the opportunity to love my child, I have slowly learned how to love others more than I ever had before.

Jesus wants us to remove the stone so He can bring life to all we thought was dead in our hearts. So many of us have lost trust in people. We have built walls to protect ourselves from pain, intimacy, and vulnerability. It is time to remove the stone and allow God to work a miracle in our lives.

42

The Sower

"AND HE TOLD THEM MANY THINGS IN PARABLES, saying: 'A sower went out to sow. And as he sowed, some seeds fell along the path, and the birds came and devoured them. Other seeds fell on rocky ground, where they did not have much soil, and immediately they sprang up, since they had no depth of soil, but when the sun rose they were scorched. And since they had no root, they withered away. Other seeds fell among thorns, and the thorns grew up and choked them. Other seeds fell on good soil and pro-duced grain, some a hundredfold, some sixty, some thirty.'"
Matthew 13:3-8

We are the soil, and it begins with us!

Planting the seed of our relationship in good soil is vital if we want to be fruitful. A strong foundation needs to be set; we must make sure our soil is treated properly. We must re-move the weeds of low self-esteem, distrust, jealousy, regret, pain, depression, and anger. Those weeds will choke the life out of our relationship. Exterminate the pests that try to find shelter in our soil, feed on our harvest, and suffocate any new growth trying to sprout.

We also need to watch out for and identify fungus gnats in our soil. The fungus gnat feeds on the hairs connected to the root of a plant; those hairs are essential for absorbing nutrients. If our source of nutrients is cut, we are left open and susceptible to toxic diseases and infections which eventually leave us infected or even lifeless. Beware of the fungus gnats trying to infest our soil, life, and mind. They are the people, things, or forces that try to cut us off or turn us against our source of support, nutrients, and power. They attempt to build barriers between us and our friends, family, and God. We need to exterminate them from our lives - pluck them out of our soil before we are left isolated, alone, dried up, and withered.

It is not enough, however, to just cut off the toxicity; we must also provide our soil, our life, ourselves, the proper treatment.

As Jesus teaches in the parable, we must plant our seed in good soil if we want it to produce. I believe we also must have a good soul if what we desire is to cultivate a loving relationship with someone else.

Before we begin treating our soil, we must plan the layout. A smart gardener does not only pay attention to the small area where the seeds are being planted; a smart gardener has foresight. He or she looks at the amount of room needed to assure that when that seed begins to grow, there is nothing around that plant to stifle its growth. We must pay the same close attention to our layout. A seed of love will have difficulty growing if its roots and vines are surrounded by negative weeds of our past and present. If we cannot move the weeds away from our life, then we have to move our life away from the weeds. Take control and responsibility for our circumstances.

Next, we should to determine what intensity of cultivation we need. Identify our weaknesses when it comes to relationships. Are we suffering from the hurt of past relationships? Maybe our weakness travels all the way back to our childhood, and we have buried it deep beneath our soil. After we have done a thorough analysis of what is in the soil of our life, plow it! Then, allow God to work through us as He prepares us to receive our blessing.

43

Battle Tested

"THEN SAUL CLOTHED DAVID with his armor. He put a helmet of bronze on his head and clothed him with a coat of mail, and David strapped his sword over his armor. And he tried in vain to go, for he had not tested them. Then David said to Saul, 'I cannot go with these, for I have not tested them.' So David put them off. Then he took his staff in his hand and chose five smooth stones from the brook and put them in his shepherd's pouch. His sling was in his hand, and he approached the Philistine." **1 Samuel 17:38-40**

David was preparing for the great battle against the Philistine, Goliath. King Saul had given him his personal armor and sword, trying to prepare David for the greatest challenge of his young life. David had already been victorious in confrontations with lions and bears, but he'd never used Saul's unfamiliar armor and weaponry. David said, *"I cannot go with these for I have not tested them."*

Like David, our destiny will come with battles. As we prepare to enter into the life God has set before us, we will face our own Goliaths, and we will encounter many challenges when we join with someone in holy matrimony.

Can you imagine what David's outcome would have been if he would have gone into battle with Saul's armor? What if he had faced the giant with a sword he had never swung or fought with a helmet he was not sure would protect him? Now, imagine yourself facing the challenges of this world with a person you are unfamiliar with. Imagine confronting the enemies of your relationship with someone you do not know. David was very familiar with his pebbles and sling. Their protection had been proven. They were battle tested.

One of the biggest parts of getting prepared for the challenges the world will throw at our relationships is having a partner who will be up for the challenge. It is so important that we attach ourselves to people that we are familiar with: people whose capabilities, commitment, and devotion have been tested. We must be like David, unwilling to enter our challenges with partners we do not know, people who are strangers to us, those who have not been tested through time.

I often say a relationship does not become serious until the couple has made it through their first argument. Attaching ourselves to people who are not ready to fight with us and for us is a huge problem when we grow impatient with prayer. In an attempt to answer our own prayers, we commit to individuals we do not know well enough. We fall in love with what they represent before we know all they are made of, the good, bad, and ugly. We often complain that people change when they actually did not.

We just never gave them enough time to reveal their true selves before we committed.

If you've been to Chicago, you know it is one of the most beautiful cities to visit during the spring or summer. The weather is comfortable; the scenery is beautiful, and there are so many great things to do and experience. If you were to fall in love with Chicago because of one season and decide to pack your bags and move there, you would have a rude awakening when the season changed. Chicago is known to have one of the harshest winters in the country—windy, freezing, and snowy. Would it be fair to hate Chicago and accuse the city of changing when the winter came?

No one likes conflict and challenges in a relationship, but we must learn to embrace conflict on some level because it is a time for testing. Challenges help us see what people are made of and to determine how strong their commitment is. Are they willing to stand and fight with us, or will they fight against us? We must use these tests to our advantage to see how much we can learn about others.

When we meet someone new, we often ask God to send a sign to tell us if he or she is the one. We look for a mystical revelation, a dream, or some prophetic word when the reality is God sends our relationships trials, tribulations, and temptations. The way we come out of these battles may be the best sign we can ever receive.

44

Build Your Relationship on the Rock

"WHY DO YOU CALL ME 'LORD, LORD,' and not do what I tell you? Everyone who comes to me and hears my words and does them, I will show you what he is like: he is like a man building a house, which dug deep and laid the foundation on the rock. And when a flood arose, the stream broke against that house and could not shake it, because it had been well built. But the one who hears and does not do them is like a man who built a house on the ground without a foundation. When the stream broke against it, immediately it fell, and the ruin of that house was great." **Luke 6:46-49**

Just as our relationships with God must be constructed on rock, the infrastructure of our relationships with our mates must also be built on a rock-solid foundation. We all know the statistics on divorce. We probably all know a couple who are currently separated, and we have all experienced breakups. If we can think back and try to remember why those relationships failed when they were flooded with the storms, waves, and whirlwinds of life, we will probably discover the source of the problem is at the origin of that relationship. Maybe we rushed into a commitment without taking the time to get to know the person, or maybe we went against what our spirit told us about them at the beginning. Maybe we began a new relationship with someone who was emotionally, mentally, and/or physically connected to someone else. Whatever the reason may have been, we can see, just like the man whose house fell because he tried to build it with no foundation, our relationships will fall if we do not use godly principles as their foundation.

If you have ever walked past a construction site where a new building was being erected, you've probably noted that the first sign construction has started is usually the presence of a gaping hole in the earth. Day after day, you look at this hole. You see workers, pipes, concrete, and trucks, but it seems like no real work is being done because there is still this huge hole. In your mind, it is taking forever to begin building because you don't consider the process started until you see something being built, but the construction workers know the most important part of building is not found in pretty doors, fancy windows, high ceilings, or the things you can see. The workers know the most important part of the structure is not what is built up; the most important part of building is what is laid down. The foundation holds up everything else.

A good foundation is what will hold up our relationships when we hit financial problems. A good foundation holds us together when we argue. A good foundation helps us work through misunderstandings, and a good foundation helps us heal when we hurt each other. The foundation is what determines whether we stand strong or fall when the storms of life come.

As you evaluate the foundation of your relationship, or, if you are thinking about entering a relationship, this is the perfect time to decide on what kind of foundation you want to build on. For a moment, think deeper than the superficial aspects of a relationship, and focus on the things that will keep you together through the test of time. Are you building on honesty, trust, faithfulness, love, loyalty, and, most importantly, are you building on God's word? The Bible has the blueprint, floor plan, and architectural layout for successful relationships, and, if you follow it, you can be sure your foundation will be properly set.

45

Your First Purpose, First Instinct

"THE LORD GOD SAID, 'It is not good for man to be alone. I will make a helper suitable for him.'" **Genesis 2:18**

The Lord created woman to be a helpmate to a man. As a woman, do you realize how much of blessing you are? You have been created to bring fulfillment where there was emptiness; a woman brings assistance in a place of need, and she has the ability to make sense out of what confuses a man. God knew the man would get some things wrong. The Lord knew man could not do it alone. He knew that even the greatest man, a man made in His own image would fall short in certain areas, and she is created to be that complement to his deficiencies.

So the question is, when your man does the inevitable and gets it wrong, what is your first instinct? Do you criticize? Do you get upset? Do you get passive aggressive and give him the silent treatment? Or do you do what God created you to do? Do you leave him to fix the mess he created, or do you help him figure out a solution?

A man once wanted to surprise his wife on a romantic getaway to a Caribbean island. He began his search and reserved the flights to stay at an all-inclusive resort. He could not wait to see the smile on her face when she found out all he had done for her. But as men do, he forgot to check on one small but important detail: the distance between the resort and airport. When they arrived on the island and discovered the airport was three hours from the resort, he began to search for rooms to stay overnight, taxis to catch, buses to transfer to, and shuttles to take to the resort. He really felt bad for this miscalculation and was trying to figure it out by himself.

After his wife listened to the details of the dilemma, she asked a simple question, "What is the difference in price, hassle, and time to pay a car service to drive the three hours versus catching a cab to the bus, then bus to a hotel, then shuttle from the hotel to the resort?" They took the car service and saw parts of the island they would not have seen on the resort. They were able to get to the resort in good time, and they enjoyed a beautiful weekend together.

How different would their weekend have been if she had gotten frustrated with him, criticized his mistake, shut down, or given him the silent treatment? Her first instinct was to help him, support him, and collaborate with him to find a solution. God made woman the original first responder. She was created to breathe life into a dying situation, stop the bleeding, and stitch up what the man had torn. Embrace your purpose; walk in your natural state, and be the blessing you were created to be to your spiritual soul mate.

46

Through the Storms

"BUT IMMEDIATELY JESUS SPOKE to them, saying, 'Take heart; Do not be afraid.' And Peter answered him, 'Lord, if it is you, command me to come to you on the water.' He said, 'Come.' So Peter got out of the boat and walked on the water and came to Jesus. But when he saw the wind, he was afraid, and beginning to sink he cried out, 'Lord, save me.' Jesus immediately reached out his hand and took hold of him, saying to him, 'O you of little faith, why did you doubt?' And when they got into the boat, the wind ceased." **Matthew 14:27-32**

"O you of little faith, why did you doubt?"

Are you having a "Peter moment" in your relationship? When the winds get strong, when the tides of our relationship get rough, and when the boat begins to rock, do we lose our faith? Do we begin to think about abandoning ship? Just like Peter, our faith in relationships can be very fickle. Our trust can be unstable. Our commitment wavers. It can all begin to sink at any hint of discomfort or trouble. It is always easy to show love when the waters are calm, when the sun is shining, and when a refreshing breeze is blowing. The true test of our faith and commitment comes when the waves begin to crash against the foundation of our relationship.

We do not like to have conflict in our relationships, but conflict is inevitable. It will occur when two individuals attempt to come together as one. The question is, how will we respond when the rapids begin to rage? Will we go wherever the wind blows us, or will we stand firmly in our faith with God and our mate? Will we be able to navigate our way through the storm, and back to the safety of the shore?

When we encounter a rough patch, we cannot take our focus off God and turn our attention to the horror of our circumstances as Peter did. We cannot turn away from our mate and Jesus and seek out comfort and guidance from others outside our relationship. The love triangle between you, your mate, and Jesus Christ is strong enough to take you through any storm.

When we feel our relationship is sinking and when we think we are about to drown in our problems, we need to do as Peter did and scream out, "Lord, save us!" Then He will grab our hands and bring us to safety.

47

Launch Out

"AND HE ENTERED INTO ONE OF THE SHIPS, which was Simon's, and prayed him that he would thrust out a little from the land. And he sat down, and taught the people out of the ship. Now when he had left speaking, he said unto Simon, 'Launch out into the deep, and let down your nets for a draught.' And Simon answering said unto him, 'Master, we have toiled all the night, and have taken nothing: nevertheless at thy word I will let down the net.' And when they had this done, they enclosed a great multitude of fishes: and their net brake. And they beckoned unto their partners, which were in the other ship, that they should come and help them. And they came, and filled both the ships, so that they began to sink." **Luke 5:3-7**

In the scripture, Simon Peter was fishing in his boat all night, but his efforts were unsuccessful. Then Jesus spoke to him and instructed him to *"Launch out into the deep, and let down your nets for a catch."* When Simon obeyed, he received the fullness of God's blessing.

When I speak to single men, I often hear the disdain in their voices as they explain how there are not many women who are worthy of being a wife. They complain about the morals and mindsets of the women they encounter. A great lesson could be learned through this scripture to help address this issue. As men, we to have to launch out and go deeper if we are to find the catch God has for us.

As we sit in the midst of our singleness, looking and searching to catch our blessing, we become doubtful just as Peter did. We get frustrated each time we encounter an individual who seems promising but ends up disappointing. We continue the tiresome task of toiling through a batch that is unsuitable and/or unavailable. Our tendency is to say there is a lack of quality women. But do we ever consider that we just might be searching in the wrong places? So many men think that we will find who God has for us in the shallow areas that we have the tendency to search. Just as Jesus told Peter Simon to launch out into the deep, we also have to launch out; because we will never find the blessings we are looking for in places where we have grown accustomed to looking. Peter could not catch his blessing in the shallow parts of the waters, and we cannot expect to find our "good thing" in the places we looked before Jesus called us to follow Him.

What shallow places are we searching? Is it the same old neighborhood bar or club we frequented before we got saved? Are we visiting the same websites? Are we searching in the shallow things that the world glorifies—the cars, the clothing, big houses, and pretty faces? Discovering a good mate is similar to the differences we find between snorkeling and deep sea diving. When snorkeling, we stay on the surface; there isn't much to see other than the occasional seaweed floating by. But, in deep sea diving, we are able to experience the true beauty of the ocean. We see all the tropical fish and plants that live well below the surface.

God has someone for us, but we have to look past what we can see with the naked eye. If our soulmates were in the places we have always searched, then wouldn't we have found them by now? But, like Peter, we continue searching in these shallow places, hoping to catch a blessing, but we will keep coming up empty until we move in the direction Jesus is telling us to go.

Jesus is telling us that we have to go deeper. We have to stop looking at the shallow things that once attracted us.

Jesus launches deep inside a person's heart, faith, integrity, loyalty, and commitment into the things we cannot see on the surface of shallow waters. We must do the same if we want to find the blessing that God has waiting for us.

48

Hour of Temptation

"AND CAME TO THE DISCIPLES and found them sleeping. And he said to Peter, 'So, could you not watch with me for one hour? Watch and pray that you may not enter temptation. The spirit is indeed willing, but the flesh is weak.'" **Matthew 26:40-41**

In this scripture, Jesus and His disciples were in Gethsemane. Gethsemane was the place where Jesus cried out to God. It was a place of great agony and despair for Christ, a very pressing place. Gethsemane was where He went as the hour of His betrayal drew nearer. As Jesus prayed to His Father, asking; *"My Father, if it be possible, let this cup pass from me; nevertheless, not as I but as you will* (Matthew 26:39)," the disciples fell asleep after being told to *"Watch and pray that you may not enter temptation."* They were unable to stand guard. They became comfortable, and, during the hour of temptation, the disciples slept. In an instant, they were caught off guard. They were totally defenseless when the enemy showed up to arrest the Lord.

The disciples fell victim to their temptation, and the steps to Jesus' betrayal, crucifixion, and death were put into motion. As single Christians, we have the same orders that were given to the disciples on that night in Gethsemane: "Watch and pray that you may not fall into temptation." As we wait for a spiritual soulmate, we are challenged by the entice-ments of the world. There are many temptations that try to lead us away from God's will and God's way. The moment we fall asleep is the moment we will face our own hour of temptation.

Jesus gave the disciples two safeguards we can use against the desires that tantalize us: "Remain prayerful and watch-ful." The civil war between our spirit and our flesh is some-thing we all experience. The power of the flesh is in its weak-ness; meaning once we get caught in the snare of temptation, the hold can be extremely powerful. Many of us ask how we can stay strong, patient, and obedient as we wait for God. A valuable lesson can be learned through what happened in Gethsemane as the disciples waited for Jesus. Through that lesson, we can learn how to strengthen our line of defense so we are not caught off guard when we are confronted with our hours of temptation.

There are several temptations we face every day. No mat-ter how much we set our spirits and minds to fight against the things that tempt us, we still struggle with certain thoughts, feelings, and behaviors. We all are weak in different areas of our singleness. For some of us, it's sex. For others, it's a no good ex; for some, it might be the feeling of loneliness. Whatever it may be, Satan knows exactly what our weak-nesses are, and his mission is to keep us tempted, hoping we will fail our mission to stay obedient to God's statutes for singles.

Temptation is everywhere: it is present in the media, on the internet, on magazine stands, and in our own minds. As we wait and seek for a special person to enter our lives, the things that tempt us to give into our fleshly desires are also seeking an opportunity to enter into our lives.

In Gethsemane, Jesus Himself was in a weak moment and asked God to go against His own will by requesting, *"Let this cup pass from me,"* but through prayer He was able to say, *"Nevertheless, not as I, but as you will."* Where is our Gethsemane? Where are we weakest? How do we keep ourselves strong when we are feeling tempted, weak, and vulnerable?

We are told to watch and pray. Being watchful is more than taking a glance; we have to watch for temptation the way a gazelle sits alertly and watches for its attacker. Temptation attacks through the things we love. Satan knows our weaknesses; he attacked Jesus through His own disciple, Judas. We cannot be on the watch for temptation if we are not real about our weaknesses.

If you lose your inhibition when you drink, do not think you can go out and socially drink and then properly handle advances from people you find attractive. Don't lie in bed with the opposite sex and say, "We are just going to watch television." When we pretend we have no vulnerabilities, we are only setting ourselves up for defeat. We must prepare for temptations.

On our jobs, we have safety plans in place for emergencies. We need to also create an emergency plan in case of temptation. When we enter into a courtship, we should discuss ways to avoid temptation: go out in groups, set a curfew, and establish off-limit topics. We must prepare before we find ourselves in compromising positions. Most importantly, we need to stay prayerful. Satan may know our weaknesses, but God knows our abilities. The Word tells us in 1 Corinthians 10:13, *"No temptation has over taken you that is not common to man. God is faithful, and he will not let you be tempted beyond your ability, but with the temptation he will also provide the way of escape, that you may be able to endure it."*

49

It's Never Too Late

"*SO WHEN EVEN WAS COME, the lord of the vineyard saith unto his steward, 'Call the laborers, and give them their hire, beginning from the last unto the first.' And when they came that were hired about the eleventh hour, they received every man a penny. But when the first came, they supposed that they should have received more; and they likewise received every man a penny. And when they had received it, they murmured against the goodman of the house, Saying, 'These last have wrought but one hour, and thou hast made them equal unto us, which have borne the burden and heat of the day.' But he answered one of them, and said, 'Friend, I do thee no wrong: didst not thou agree with me for a penny? Take that thine is, and go thy way: I will give unto this last, even as unto thee. Is it not lawful for me to do what I will with mine own? Is thine eye evil, because I am good? So the last shall be first, and the first last: for many be called, but few chosen.'*" **Matthew 20:8-16**

God's blessing, grace, and favor is not first come first served. Nothing is ever too late for Him, and when you put your faith and trust in Him, you will realize that nothing is ever too late for you.

When it comes to love and relationships, many of us miss the true blessing of a loving, honest, fulfilling, God-guided relationship because we enter into a race against time. We begin to think too much time has passed, that our best years are behind us, or that we missed the chance at love. As, the verse says, *"So the last shall be first, and the first last."*

God is the creator and controller of time, and we cannot allow negative messages to pollute our hopes for love, or the fear of timing infiltrate our minds as we get older, experience a divorce, or have a long-term relationship end. We cannot allow ourselves to feel we are running out of time. Self-inflicted pressure does not usually lead us to give up on love; instead it makes us rush it. We begin speeding up the process of building a solid foundation in our relationships. We rush our decision making, and don't take the time to really get to know the individual. We sacrifice our bodies, hearts, and souls, all because of our fear of time. Before we know it, we are moving at our speed and not God's speed.

We see our friends getting married, having children, building their families, and, from our perspective, they seem happy. It may begin to feel like we will be the last ones to meet our spiritual soul mates. We may even begin to doubt if we will meet them at all. The feeling grows even stronger when we are not the last laborers who showed up at the eleventh hour, but we were actually the first laborers who have been working in the vineyard since sunrise. We feel we have been committed and obedient. We've made personal changes and done what we believe is pleasing to God, but we are not pleased with what God has been doing for us. We compare ourselves to others, and we begin to feel they do not deserve their blessings. We start murmuring and complaining; we question why God hasn't sent us our soul mates. As we see in the parable, however, it is never too late for us to receive the full blessing God has prepared for us. God is gracious to the last as He is to the first.

50

Private Testimony

"AND HE TOOK THE BLIND MAN BY THE HAND, and led him out of the town; and when he had spit on his eyes, and put his hands upon him, he asked him if he saw ought. And he looked up, and said, 'I see men as trees, walking.' After that he put his hands again upon his eyes, and made him look up: and he was restored, and saw every man clearly. And he sent him away to his house, saying, 'neither go into the town, nor tell it to any in the town.'" **Mark 8:23-26**

In these verses, we see Jesus performing another miraculous act. He brings sight to the blind. This is just one of the many magnificent works of our Lord. But, there is something a little different about this blessing: Jesus' actions afterward might seem peculiar to us. He sent the man away and told him not to go back into the town he came from or tell anyone in the town about the miracle. Why would Jesus prevent the man from spreading the word about his blessing? Why would He instruct the man to keep his mouth shut, restrict his testimony, and tell him not to even go back to the town he'd found him in?

Some say Jesus didn't want the attention it would bring; others say Jesus did not want jealousy to stir up among those in the village, and there are others who say the Pharisees who lived there would try to cause trouble after seeing the blessing. Just as Jesus instructed the blind man to keep quiet about his blessing of sight, sometimes we are also better off keeping quiet when He blesses us with the relationship we prayed for.

Sometimes, the people we think will be the happiest that God finally sent us the man or woman we prayed for are like those found in the village of the blind man. The ones we shared our loneliness with, who kept us encouraged, and watched us go in and out of bad relationships are not always able to celebrate our happiness when God allows us to meet our spiritual soulmate. It is shameful, but it's a reality. At times, we have to be careful who we talk to about the goodness and virtue of our mate. In the scripture, Jesus told the blind man not to speak of his blessing to the same people who had brought him to Jesus to get healed. Jesus sees the heart, and He knows who is really for us and who isn't. Through prayer and supplication, He will reveal who those individuals are in our lives.

There are several examples of when jealous naysayers made attempts to hinder the blessings of others. In Matthew, when Jesus cast out demons, people said He did in the spirit of Beelzebul, or when He healed others, they said it was unlawful because He did it on the Sabbath. This shows us there will always be someone trying to poke holes in your blessing. They'll tell you about what your mate "used to" do, who they "used to" be with, or how they "used to" treat someone else.

It is very important to have good counsel in your life and to find those who truly support you and your relationship. Pray for discernment so God can bring those people into your life.

51

Good Counsel

"NOW THE SERPENT WAS MORE CRAFTY than any other beast of the field that the Lord God had made. He said to the woman, 'Did God actually say, 'You shall not eat of any tree in the garden'?' And the woman said to the serpent, 'We may eat of the fruit of the trees in the garden, but God said, 'You shall not eat of the fruit of the tree that is in the midst of the garden, neither shall you touch it, lest you die.'' But the serpent said to the woman, 'You will not surely die. For God knows that when you eat of it your eyes will be opened, and you will be like God, knowing good and evil.'' **Genesis 3:1-5**

Be careful who you talk to about your relationship. In these verses, we read about the fall of mankind. We see Eve conversing with Satan, and he deceptively convinces her to go against the will of God, betray the trust of her husband, and to rebel against the goodness of her own heart. We are familiar with how the story ends. Adam and Eve's relationship with God and each other was tarnished. The paradise they enjoyed was shut off from them, and a generational curse followed their family from that day on.

It all started with a conversation. Eve sought counsel from someone who was not in favor of the betterment of her relationship with God or her husband. While we wait for God to lead us to the person He has prepared for us, we must be careful who we ask for relationship advice. It is important to develop discernment so we can wisely choose good counsel; voices who will help us better prepare ourselves for our spiritual soul mates instead of misguiding us to do things that can jeopardize our blessing.

Even before we are blessed with that special person, we must learn to surround ourselves with individuals who are for us, those who support the institution of a godly marriage, and who have our best interests at heart.

As we prepare ourselves for who God has for us, we must seek counsel from individuals who will help guide us toward becoming a better mate to whomever God will send. Our experiences are not so different from Eve's when we trust people who are false friends. These are the people we confide in about relationship issues; they are the ones we open up to about what's going on in our hearts and allow to hook us up with others. What makes them false friends is when we find out they have told others the things we told them in confidence. They are the people in our lives who are envious of the relationships we have, or the ones who try to couple us with a girlfriend or boyfriend who has none of the qualities we told them we wanted in a spiritual soul mate. These "friends" can be as crafty as the serpent was with Eve, and, just like with Eve, taking their advice could lead to the destruction of what we hold dear.

52

Serving Our Purpose

"AND SEEING FROM AFAR A FIG TREE having leaves, he went to see if perhaps he would find something on it. When he came to it he found nothing but leaves, for it was not in season for figs. In response Jesus said to it, 'Let no one eat fruit from you ever again.'" **Mark 11:13-14**

This scripture speaks of a fig tree that was cursed by Jesus. The tree was created to provide fruit for the hungry. But, when Jesus found Himself in need of its fruit, it had none. The tree gave the appearance of being ready for harvest. It was covered with leaves, fully grown, and seemed to have reached its maturity where its fruit would be ripe and ready to eat, but this was not the case. As a result, Jesus cursed the fig tree, saying, "Let no one eat fruit from you ever again." He did not curse it out of frustration or anger; Jesus cursed the tree because it suggested great promise but failed to serve its purpose.

This scripture reminds me of how many of us men, including myself, have failed to fulfill our purpose in relationships. And as a result of that unfulfilled purpose, we find ourselves in the same predicament as the fig tree. We give the appearance of being ready to provide for the needs of a woman. We look fully grown; we dress like a man. We walk like a man, and even talk like a man, but we fail to fulfill the purpose we were created for. Jesus' actions are a warning and lesson against the dangers of spiritual fruitlessness.

As men, there is a lesson to learn from this tree. Let's ask ourselves, how many relationships have withered away due to our lack of fruitfulness? How many individuals have we disappointed because we have not fulfilled our purpose? The curse that no one should eat fruit from the tree can be translated to us never finding that spiritual soul mate if we do not learn to fulfill our purpose.

Be fruitful and multiply; tend and keep. Those were God's orders to man when he was placed in the Garden of Eden. He is clear on our purpose. In our relationships with women, our purpose does not change. We need to be "fruitful and multiply" the good that God created her to be. We should tend to her needs and keep her as she is our own. God placed one of His most precious creations in our care. So let us take a self-inventory. For those of us who are seeking spiritual soul mates also and for those who feel they have already found one, where are we in the areas of being fruitful, multiplying, tending, and keeping God's creation? We have been given a responsibility to do these things for those who are in our care. We have fooled ourselves into thinking that being fruitful and multiplying stops at making babies.

It is time for us to fulfill our purpose as men in all of our relationships. We must prove our self-faithfulness with the smaller responsibilities we are given, such as being a brother, being a son, being a good worker, and being an example to others. We must show we are being fruitful, multiplying, tending, and keeping those relationships as He has ordered us to, and, maybe then, we will be prepared to be fruitful, multiply, tend to, and keep the one God has prepared for us.

53

Battle of the Sexes

"You, my brothers and sisters, were called to be free. But do not use your freedom to indulge the flesh; rather, serve one another humbly in love. For the entire law is fulfilled in keeping this one command: 'Love your neighbor as yourself.' If you bite and devour each other, watch out or you will be destroyed by each other." **Galatians 5:13-15**

Men are not from Mars, and women are not from Venus. We all come from the same Father, same flesh, and same bone. The world would lead us to believe we are so different that we could never live in harmony with each other, and that idea is absurd.

The verse reads, *"If you bite and devour each other, watch out or you will be destroyed by each other."* Men and women seem to be at odds. We argue and debate over gender roles in society, relationships, and almost every aspect of life. This is a dangerous pattern to fall into as singles. These types of interactions create a mental and emotional wall toward the opposite sex while our hearts and souls continue to yearn for connection. This internal conflict results in confusion, plants seeds of constant contradiction, and establishes cat-and-mouse, push-and pull types of relationships.

In some cases, years of mistreatment from the opposite sex forms our perception about them. In other cases, we may have been taught by parents or society that a man or woman is only good for certain things but not needed for anything else. Or possibly, we have seen negative interactions between husbands and wives and other men and women for most of our lives. Whether we develop this scorn from our experiences or our ignorance comes from being misinformed, these are wrong perceptions of how God wants us to interact as brothers and sisters.

Until we are able to love each other as He has commanded, we will always struggle to truly love the men or women who enter our lives. That scorn, distrust, competitiveness, ignorance, and rebellion will always prevent us from developing intimate relationships.

54

Due Diligence

"Do not be hasty in the laying on of hands, nor take part in the sins of others; keep yourself pure... The sins of some men are conspicuous, going before them to judgment, but the sins of others appear later. So also good works are conspicuous, and even those that are not cannot remain hidden." **1 Timothy 5:22, 24**

In the text, Paul is giving instructions to Timothy on how to select good leaders for the church. In addition to the many other qualifications listed in previous chapters for holding positions as a bishop, a minister, and a deacon, in chapter five, Paul advises Timothy on how to identify good qualifications for choosing the right leaders. Paul teaches, *"Do not be hasty"; "Keep yourself pure"; "The sins of some men are conspicuous/obvious,"* and *"The sins of others appear later,"* as do their "good works." The advice given for selecting good church leadership is also sound advice for selecting good leadership for our lives, our homes, and our relationships. Paul is trying to teach us the importance of doing our due diligence.

Once we are ready and open to receive our spiritual soul mates, due diligence is crucial, and this scripture provides helpful guidance through that vital process.

Paul stated, *"Don't be hasty."* Basically, he is saying do not rush into quick decisions about leadership. The best practice is to take your time. We should also take that advice and not act hastily as we prepare to start down a road that will lead to a lifelong partnership. We should be cautious and careful with our selections. Do not be afraid to do some fair investigating, and make sure to get spiritual confirmation of their qualifications.

"Keep yourself pure." Doing our due diligence is a way of keeping ourselves pure and innocent from the sins of others. If someone has the responsibility of selecting a good leader, but neglects to complete a thorough evaluation of the individual he or she chooses and as a result that person misleads others, should not the person who made the selection be held partially responsible for the outcome? Being deceived and lied to is one thing, but if the person we chose to join with was allowed to get a free pass without our careful examination, or if they showed red flags and we chose to ignore them, we are not totally innocent, and we share in their sin. Therefore, one way to keep ourselves pure and free from blame is to do a good comprehensive assessment at the beginning to learn what a person is like instead of being surprised when we begin to discover things we overlooked.

"The sins of some men are conspicuous." Paul is teaching Timothy, that there will be some whose sinful ways are out

in the open and easily detectable. Those individuals are not even qualified to be considered for leadership. This lesson is easily transferable to our personal lives. We cannot ignore red flags we clearly see or make excuses for inconsistencies. We cannot allow attraction to lead us down a road of pain and disappointment. We cannot fool ourselves into believing we can change someone. We cannot rationalize someone's sinful behavior as a manifestation of hurt emotions. Those individuals are not fit to lead us.

We must do a better job of asking the important questions and looking for the important qualities. I was once told, "The things that we look for in a fun and attractive date, may not be the same thing we look for in a lifelong mate." With the divorce rate being what it is, and the reasons for divorces moving further and further away from what God allows, it is so important for us to go through the process of really getting to know someone and building a relationship before committing to a stranger.

55

Focus, Discipline, Hard Work

"NO SOLDIER GETS ENTANGLED IN CIVILIAN PUR-SUITS, since his aim is to please the one who enlisted him. An athlete is not crowned unless he competes according to the rules. It is the hard-working farmer who ought to have the first share of the crops." **2 Timothy 2:4-6**

In the text, Paul is writing to Timothy to encourage him and to explain the characteristics he needs and the qualities he must develop in order to withstand what he will face as he continues in his journey as an ambassador for Christ.

Paul uses as examples: the focus and obedience of soldier, the discipline of an athlete, and the hard work of a farmer. This is to illustrate the level of strength and commitment we must have as witnesses of Jesus. "The Soldier": he does not involve himself in matters that are not consistent with his orders and duties. "The Athlete": his discipline to the rules is what crowns him victorious at the end. "The Farmer": his hard work leads to a great harvest.

As I studied these individuals, I realized their attributes are very applicable and much needed in our relationships.

If we want to receive the full reward God has for our relationships, we should desire the strength and tenacity needed
to stand the test of time. As we prepare for our spiritual
soul mates we should strive to develop the focus of a solder
and the discipline of an athlete. We should also work hard
to cultivate healthy relationships in the same way a farmer
works hard at cultivating a good harvest.

Every couple should have a shared goal and a common
mission. In order for that mission to be accomplished, a
couple must execute their respective duties with the focus
and obedience of a soldier. In every squadron, each solider
has a position; every solider has his or her responsibility,
but each individual is working toward the shared mission of
the platoon. A distraction by one can put the entire platoon
in jeopardy. The same goes for couples. They have to stay
focused on their joint missions.

If we want our relationships to be successful, we cannot
allow ourselves to get distracted by outside people, outside
problems, or outside things that will take us away from what
have decided to accomplish together. We must have a clear
mission. We should have a clear plan for our relationship,
as well as a plan b, which safeguards us during times when
things don't go as planned.

We are often shocked when our relationships do not work
out or are not blessed. But how can we be shocked when
our behaviors during the relationship are not disciplined by
the rules God has set for us? Just as an athlete has rules
for competition, we have rules for engaging in relationships.

When an athlete breaks the rules of the game he or she is disqualified; likewise, when we break the rules of engagement, our relationships usually become dismantled. As we prepare ourselves for a mate, we have to always remember what God expects of us. We cannot blatantly defy what God expects of us sexually, socially, spiritually, or behaviorally and still hope for the relationship to be blessed. If we adopt the discipline of an athlete and follow the rules, then victory will be a guarantee, because God promised that.

We hear it all the time, "Relationships are hard work." Like everything else in life, when we put in the work, we will see the results. Even when things seem to come naturally, we have to work to maintain it. We must work to maintain and develop good communication. We must work to stay committed. We must work to be the best mate we can be. We also have to work to make good things even better. We cannot rest on our laurels. If we work like a farmer, the outcome will always be in our favor.

56

Impressions

"SO RUTH THE MOABITESS SAID TO NAOMI, 'Please let me go to the field, and glean head of grain after him in whose sight I may find favor.' And she said to her, 'Go, my daughter.' Then she left, and went and gleaned in the field after the reapers. And she happened to come to the part of the field belonging to Boaz, who was of the family of Elimelech. Now behold, Boaz came from Bethlehem, and said to the reapers, 'The Lord be with you!' And they answered him, 'The Lord bless you!' Then Boaz said to his seat who was in charge of the reapers, 'Whose young woman is this' So the servant who was in charge of the reapers answered and said, 'It it's the young Moabite woman who came back with Naomi from the country of Moab.' And she said, 'Please let me glean and let me follow after the reapers among the sheaves.' So she came and has continued from morning until now, though she rested a little in the house." **Ruth 2:2-7**

We have all heard the saying, "You only get one chance to make a first impression." I really believe that this saying holds a lot of truth, and this truth is seen in the relationship we read about between Ruth and Boaz. Their encounter illustrates the importance of making a good first impression, and how that can possibly lead to the blessing that awaits us, just as it did for Ruth.

In the scripture, we see a woman who is seeking to be noticed and gain favor from a man, a good and worthy man. We read how Ruth puts herself in a position that will increase her chances to be recognized by Boaz and gain his favor, which leads to her becoming his wife. Let's examine the approach Ruth took to get noticed, and how her first introduction into Boaz's life led to a great blessing.

"Please let me go to the field, and glean head of grain after him in whose sight I may find favor." As a woman who wants to gain favor from a good man, how are you choosing to attract his admiration and attention?

In the story, Ruth chooses to show her worth through her work and not through her skirt. She went to his field and gleaned, gathering the leftover grain, which the reapers of the harvest had dropped and left behind. This was a very slow, tedious, and laborious process. Like the virtuous woman described in Proverbs 31, Ruth worked with willing hands, with the fruit of her hands she planted a vineyard, she put her hands to the distaff, and her hands hold the spindle, all examples of how hard working she was. Ruth made a choice that the first impression she would make on Boaz would be her diligently helping in his field. She did this subtly, without him knowing. By doing this, she showed she would support his goals and be an asset to him. Ruth made his mission a part of her ministry, and there is nothing more needed by a strong and progressive man than a woman who helps and supports him.

The intelligent and virtuous woman understands the importance that a man like Boaz puts on his work and business. She knows that showing herself as a helpmate is the way to gain favor and also a way to his heart. A lady should always be aware of the impression she is leaving on a man. If the attempt to gain attention, love, and favor is done by using her outward beauty instead of her inner strength, the attention and infatuation she receives will eventually fade away, just like the pretty face or sexy body used to get it.

In this overly sexualized society we live in, there is a pressure to be the "hottest" or "sexiest." The world wants you to believe a woman's value is found in the roundness of her derriere, the perkiness of her breasts, or the curve of her hips. Though God has made each woman beautiful in her own way, and it is a great thing to appreciate and be confident in that gift from God, solely relying on physical appearance to make an impression on a man will only impress his sexual and lustful side, never his loving and committed side.

Ruth showed she would add great value to Boaz's life. She delighted in her work and was diligent in her labor. Support, devotion, and encouragement are the keys to any man's heart. Ruth's first choice to show her worth through her work drew Boaz to her and made him love her. When she washed, anointed, and clothed herself in her beautiful garments to meet him on the threshing floor that was only the icing on the cake.

57

What Makes Him Ready?

"THE LORD GOD TOOK THE MAN and put him in the Garden of Eden to work it and keep it...Then the Lord God said, 'It is not good that the man should be alone; I will make him a helper fit for him...' The man gave names to all livestock and to the birds of the heavens and to every beast of the field. But for Adam there was not found a helper fit for him. So the Lord God caused a deep sleep to fall upon the man, and while he slept took one of his ribs and closed up its place with flesh. And the rib that the Lord God had taken from the man he made into a woman and brought her to the man." **Genesis 2:15-22**

Most of us are familiar with the creation story. We often have debates on our purposes and roles as men or women in a relationship or marriage based off what we read in Genesis 2. Men and women get caught up in different interpretations of this passage; we dissect the verses to fit our perceptions. We start focusing so much on what a man should be in the marriage that we forget the fact that what a man is before the marriage is equally important.

Verse fifteen reads, *"The Lord God took the man and put him in the Garden of Eden to work it and keep it."* Notice what this verse is telling us. Before God made a wife for Adam, he was given responsibilities. Before God felt Adam needed a woman by his side, he gave him a job to do. Before Adam was blessed with an assistant, he had to prove he was a leader, a hard worker, and a keeper of God's creation. So, before focusing on what type of husband you would be, or what type of partner a man would be to you, examine what type of man he is while he is still single.

It is not a coincidence God did these things in a specific order. The transition from boyhood to manhood is not strictly based on age, physical stature, or sexual conquest. A boy becomes a man when he proves that he can be responsible for himself and others. When he shows commitment to whatever he decides to take on, when all of his dealings are done with integrity and honesty, and when he is disciplined enough to stick to God's plan. A man is capable of carrying the load on his own; his wife should only be there to make the load lighter.

The following rationales are just a few of the many reasons I have heard used to explain why a man should become a husband: "I'm not getting any younger." "We've been together this long; we might as well get married." "He has a good job." "My family loves him." Well, none of those reasons tells you what kind of man he is. If your measuring stick for what makes a man ready for marriage is any different than what God used to measure Adam's preparedness for Eve, then there is a strong possibility you will find your man is not ready. God made a man responsible before He made him a husband, and that is great criteria for everyone to use.

58

Love from Loved Ones

"AND SAMSON WENT DOWN TO TIMNATH, and saw a woman in Timnath of the daughters of the Philistines. And he came up, and told his father and his mother, and said 'I have seen a woman in Timnath of the daughters of the Philistines: now therefore get her for me to wife.' Then his father and his mother said unto him, 'Is there not a woman among the daughters of thy brethren, or among all my people, that you can take a wife of the uncircumcised Philistines?' And Samson said unto his father; 'Get her for me; for she pleases me well.'" **Judges 14:1-3**

Samson married a woman he saw in Timnath, even though his mother and father urged him to find someone else. He ignored the fact that she was a Philistine, an enemy and oppressor of his people, and, most importantly, he was un-deterred by the law of God, which forbade Israelites from marrying outside of their nation. Samson was determined to be with this woman. He refused the protection and advice of those who were close to him, and he decided to follow his lustful desires.

If we continue reading this chapter, we learn this marriage eventually leads to Samson being deceived and manipulated by this woman. She cheats on him with his best man and conspires with his enemies. Due to Samson's direct disobedience to God's word and his refusal of good and loving advice, he becomes enraged by what transpires in his relationship, and he destroys acres of land and kills thousands of people. This results in Samson having to run for his life and hide in caves.

As we travel this journey of love, waiting and seeking our spiritual soul mates, we will meet people who will ignite lustful desires in us. We may develop feelings for people who do not have our best interests at heart, and we may get caught in a battle between what we want and what we need. During those times, we can become blinded by attraction, distracted by our emotions, and unable to see the true fruit of individuals. We can lose ourselves in our efforts to be with someone. However, be assured that in those times, God places people around us who can provide good counsel and help us see things and people from a perspective we cannot see when our emotions, minds, and spirits are at war with each other.

Samson had the advice and protection of his parents and God's word, but he refused to take advantage of either one. How many times have we refused the advice of a loved one who tried to give us insight on a relationship we were in? Did we even take their advice into consideration, or did we instantly get defensive, rebellious, and try to prove everyone wrong? Did we hear them out, or did we decide to ignore them and follow our desires, no matter how far off track they took us?

As we continue on this journey, we must remember we cannot do it all alone. We have family, friends, loved ones, clergy, and counselors, from whom we can seek good counsel about relationships and love. Let us take advantage of those God has placed in our lives that can help us better differentiate our wants from our needs.

59

Stay True to You

When David returned home to bless his household, Michal daughter of Saul came to meet him and said, "How the king of Israel has distinguished himself today, going around half-naked in full view of the slave girls of his servants as any vulgar fellow would!" David said to Michal, "It was before the Lord, who chose me rather than your father or anyone from his house when he appointed me ruler over the Lord's people Israel-I will celebrate before the Lord." 2 Samuel 6:20-21

The backdrop of this interaction between David and his wife Michal takes place when King David is on a journey back to his home with the ark of the Lord. King David was so full of joy that he was dancing and praising the Lord in the middle of the street the entire way home. When he arrives home, his wife Michal sarcastically approaches him and says, *"How the king of Israel has distinguished himself today."* Her misery was searching for company by attempting to steal the joy of her husband.

Have you ever been in a relationship where you felt that you had to alter who God made you to be in order to not offend, upset, or outdo your mate? Have you ever been with someone who tries to steal your joy or blow your light out as soon as they see a small glimmer?

In this scripture that is what we see happening between King David and Michal. Her anger stops her from celebrating a huge moment in the life of her husband, her people, and herself. The person that God has prepared for you will never stand in the way of who God is preparing you to be. If you find yourself being influenced to do things such as: change the positive things that you like about yourself, neglect things that God has placed on your heart; or act in sin, you must ask yourself, "Is this the one that God has prepared for me?"

David did not allow the words of his wife to discourage him or change him. As we journey toward our own soul mates we will come across many individuals that will say and do things to try to derail us off of the path that God has put us on. There will be individuals that might leave us when they realize how serious we actually are about our walk. But don't be disappointed and don't get frustrated, and do not be like me.

There have been times when I have dimmed my own light. I have tried to minimize my own excitement for God to avoid alienating someone or to make someone that I was interested more comfortable and accepting of me. I had to come to the revelation that the one that is for me will love me as well the Christ that is in me, and I should never let their negative attitude toward my beliefs effect my positive perspective on life.

So be true to who you are. Celebrate what God has put in you. And never let anyone steal your joy.

60

Strength to Endure

"THEREFORE, SINCE WE ARE SURROUNDED by so great a cloud of witnesses, let us also lay aside every weight, and sin which clings so closely, and let us run with endurance the race that is set before us, looking to Jesus, the founder and perfecter of our faith, who for the joy that was set before him endured the cross, despising the shame, and is seated at the right hand of the throne of God. Consider him who endured from sinners such hostility against himself, so that you may not grow weary or fainthearted. In your struggle against sin you have not yet resisted to the point of shedding your blood."
Hebrews 12:1-4

When we act with God's purpose in mind, we can endure all the pains and struggles we encounter during the journey. We cannot allow the heartbreaks, abuse, and disappointments that come with relationships to discourage us from finding true love and happiness. We must remember the reward of opening up our hearts is greater than the risk when we find the love God wants us to have. As the scripture says, *"looking to Jesus, the founder and perfecter of our faith, who for the joy that was set before him endured the cross, despising the shame, and is seated at the right hand of the throne of God."* Jesus was able and willing to endure the shame, pain, and torture because He kept his mind on the joy of redeeming us. So, keeping our minds on the joy of finding true love can give us strength and endurance to make it through the hard times.

There will be bumps in the road during our journey, but remember they are God's way preparing us for the one He has set aside for us. We should internalize the lessons and blessings those bumps bring, and use them to grow.

As singles looking to be married, we cannot look at dating as a burden or a hassle; we need to embrace the process of meeting new people, learning new things, gaining new experiences. "For the joy that is set before," when we are appointed our lifelong mate, it is worth the wait. When we look back the obstacles we encountered along the way, they will appear as minor inconveniences when we finally meet the one who was made to love us.

61

A Call to Lead

"FOR THE HUSBAND IS THE HEAD OF THE WIFE as Christ is the head of the church, his body, of which he is the Savior. Now as the church submits to Christ, so also wives should submit to their husbands in everything." **Ephesians 5:23-24**

Leadership. This scripture may be one of the most misused and misinterpreted verses in the entire Bible, and that misapplication is usually done by us men. We have a tendency to select certain words and parts of scripture to fit our circumstances or to defend our arguments, but we neglect to look for the deeper meaning and interpretation of the verse.

The scripture gives a very specific example of the type of leadership a man should have with his wife and family. It says, *"The husband is the head of the wife as Christ is the head of the church."* As men, we must first understand what kind of leader Christ was in order for us to understand what kind of leader He is calling us to be in our families.

Ephesians does not read, "As a general is the head of the army," or "as a CEO is the head of his company." Although these forms of leaders would benefit from following the example Jesus set for leadership, they are not the examples we are to follow as men.

Jesus' leadership is many things; it is loving, sacrificial, corrective, instructive, and informative, but the one thing that stands out the most to me is that Jesus' leadership took the initiative. As men, that is the example we are called to follow.

1 John 4:19 says, *"We love because he first loved us,"* and that is the key to leadership. We must get into the practice of being the initiator of love, the initiator of prayer, the initiator of tough conversations, initiator of planning, initiator of romance, initiator of coming to a resolution, and the initiator of forgiveness. We are called to take the lead in the matters of our relationships, set examples, and take the first steps in the right direction.

Jesus did not sit back and give orders to His disciples. He led by example, and they watched him and followed in His footsteps. We are not automatically leaders because we are men; we have to earn that position. Leading is an attitude and skill we all can develop if we stay open to the teachings of Jesus. So, let's take the lead in all that is good and essential and watch our relationships grow to new heights.

62

When the Honeymoon Is Over

"THEN SATAN ANSWERED THE LORD AND SAID, 'Does Job fear God for no reason? Have you not put a hedge around him and his house and all that he has, on every side? You have blessed the work of his hands, and his possessions have increased in the land. But stretch out your and touch all that he has, and he will curse you to your face.'" **Job 1:9-11**

In the book of Job, God is having a discussion with Satan. God is pointing out one of His faithful servants, Job. He tells Satan that there is no one else like Job; he is faithful, upright, blameless, and fears God. Satan's response, paraphrased from what we read in the featured verse, is, "Of course he is faithful and blameless; he has been blessed with riches, land, and family." Satan believed that once the good times were taken away from Job he would turn against God, and prove his faith and love were weak and conditional.

Just as Job was blessed in his life, we are often blessed in our lives and relationships. When we meet someone special, it can be blissful. We enjoy the companionship, the compliments, and the kind words warm our heart. We relish in the late night phone calls and the feelings of compatibility. We feel like a fence is around the relationship, and nothing can penetrate it. Satan believed God had put a fence around Job, and that Job was only faithful because the good times were rolling in. So, I ask, when the good times are interrupted in our relationships, when we come to a heated disagreement or when the honeymoon is over, how do we respond? Do we respond in the way the enemy expects, or do we maintain our faith in each other and God, as Job did?

Job teaches us some helpful ways to deal with trying times when difficulties hit our lives, and these points are easily transferable to our relationships:

Job Had the Right Mindset

In Job 1:21, Job stated, *"The Lord gave, and the Lord hath taken away; blessed be the name of the Lord."* That was Job's initial response to the news he had lost his property, cattle, and children. He put things into perspective.

When we are faced with a problem with our mate, we have to go in with the right mindset. When we fly off the handle and begin blaming, shaming, fighting, and cursing, the situation will only get worse. We should first stop and think, "Would my mate do something to intentionally cause me pain?" "Does she or he truly love me?" Put your situation in the right perspective before you react. The majority of disagreements are due to misinterpretation and misunderstanding of our mate's intentions. Thinking first helps set the course for how the disagreement will end.

Job Said Nothing He Would Regret

"Then said his wife unto him, 'Do you still retain your integrity? Curse God, and die.' But he said unto her, 'Thou speak as one of the foolish women speaks.'" Despite the troubles Job was experiencing, he remained respectful, gracious, and loving toward God.

The kind of reaction we have when we face troubles in our relationships can be the difference between a problem starting with something as small as leaving the toilet seat up, and it turning into something huge like how you hate your mate's mother. When we say things we may regret and hit below the belt during an argument, we are no longer focused on solving the problem. Our intentions are now to hurt our mate, which never leads to anything good. Even in disagreements and disappointments, we have to learn to remain respectful and get our points across in the most loving way possible.

Job Identified Who to Tell His Problems

"I have heard many such things: miserable comforters are ye all." Job's friends who came to comfort him actually failed him. Instead of encouraging him, they ended up increasing his frustration with their sarcasm and interrogation. If we must find someone to confide in during our relational issues, we must be sure that person is truly a friend who has the right intentions for us and our relationships. Talking to the wrong

people about our problems can lead to more problems. They may give advice that is ungodly or gossip to others about things that were supposed to be held in confidence.

Job Prayed and Forgave

At the end of it all, Job's faith and trust in God were what solved his problems. God immediately changed Job's fortune when Job stopped debating with his friends and started forgiving them through prayer. Everything was restored to him, plus more.

When we are faced with tough times in our relationships, there is nothing wrong with seeking counseling, going to therapy, our talking to a trusted friend, but none of that can replace God's advice. Seek His guidance through prayer and his word; stay faithful, and trust He will help bring you through any problems you and your mate have.

63

While They Can Still Smell Them

"BUT JESUS SAID, 'LET HER ALONE. Why do you trouble her? She has done a good work for me. For you have the poor with you always, and whenever you wish you may do them good; but me you do not have always. She has done what she could. She has come beforehand to anoint my body for burial. Assuredly, I say to you, wherever this gospel is preached in the whole world, what this woman has done will be told as a memorial to her.'" **Mark 14:6-9**

In the text, Jesus was talking about Mary, the sister of Martha and Lazarus, who anointed his head with very expensive fragrance oil. The value of the oil represented a year's worth of wages for a laborer during that time. Many of the disciples responded with indignity to her act. They accused her of being wasteful; they said the money from the oil could have gone to better use. Then Jesus stepped in and said, *"She has done a good work for me."*

As I reflected on this scripture and thought about the relational implications it presented, it made me think about how important it is to show continuous love and appreciation for the people God has blessed us with. The disciples in this story were angry with Mary because they felt she could have used what she had in a better way. But Jesus reminded them, *"For you have the poor with you always, and whenever you wish you may do them good; but Me you do not have always."*

Are we making good use of the time we have with the people we love? Do we feel like there are more important things we could be doing with our energy, time, and resources than to spend it on them or with them? Do we spend hours or even days arguing or being mad at each other? To paraphrase, Jesus was saying, "She's giving me my flowers while I can smell them." The time we have with the man or woman we asked God for will not last forever. It is important we develop a sense of appreciation, celebration, and service for that person. If that person has not entered our lives yet, we can begin to train our minds to prioritize our resources for him or her.

They say, "It's the thought that counts." Mary did what she could do; she sacrificed all she had as a testament of her love for Jesus.

What can we give our mates to show them we love them? We can leave them a sweet message on a sticky note before work, or we could mail them a card that expresses our appreciation for everything they do. It's important to carve out time in our busy schedules just to be with them; let's get creative. Every effort counts, and if we are on the receiving end of those efforts we should learn to be appreciative, just like Jesus was in the story. He appreciated what Mary did for Him. He did not say her gift was not good enough; He did not compare her gesture to the gesture of others. Jesus received what Mary gave with a happy and open heart.

If we have not done anything for our significant others in a while, we should make today the day we show our appreciation, just because.

It doesn't have to be Valentine's Day, Christmas, or their birthday to do something special. Let's make the time we have with them as joyous as possible today. Give them their roses while they can still smell them, give them their hugs while they still feel them, and give them their compliments while they can still hear them. Watch how these acts enrich your relationship.

Dear Reader,

I pray you found these life lessons encouraging and empowering. To delve even deeper into the topics we discussed, I have another great read for you: helps readers to recognize the four keys to relationship readiness. It is an interactive book that has proven to be powerful to those who have read it thus far. Add it to your list, and let me know what you think by leaving a review when you finish!

Until next time,

Adama B. Bracewell, MS.

www.ready4relationship.com

www.ingramcontent.com/pod-product-compliance
Lightning Source LLC
Chambersburg PA
CBHW051819090426
42736CB00011B/1559